PIZZA DEFINED

Rev. Canon [illegible],

I hope you enjoy cooking from this little book. If not then I'll attempt one of the recipies for you.

BERNADETTE O'SHEA

Every good wish.

Bernadette.

071-64850

PIZZA DEFINED

CONTEMPORARY AND CLASSICAL INTERPRETATIONS OF PIZZA, CALZONE AND FOCACCIA

BERNADETTE O'SHEA

PHOTOGRAPHY BY MIKE O'TOOLE

ESTRAGON PRESS

FIRST PUBLISHED IN 1997 BY ESTRAGON PRESS, DURRUS, COUNTY CORK

ISBN 1 874076 24 3

EDITOR: SALLY McKENNA

ART DIRECTOR: NICK CANN

FOOD STYLING: ANNE MARIE TOBIN

COLOUR SEPARATIONS BY PENTACOLOUR

PRINTED BY COLOUR BOOKS LTD

COVER SHOT: ST TOLA GOAT'S CHEESE WITH GOAT'S CHEESE & LEEK PIZZA

DEDICATED TO

Margaret my beautiful mother,

my sister Goretti, my brothers J.J. & James,

friends Francie and Charlie & my nephews Kevin and Neal,

and the great memory of Dad, Donal & Georgie

with love and thanks

WITH THANKS

Thank you to the great people who worked with me in Truffles, too many to mention, but I owe you all a debt of gratitude and I will single out a few: Rosa Borras, Cathy Clarke, Emanuel Crozier, Aoife Henry, Michelle Henry, James Jackson, Ruth Johnson, Cathy Jordan, Sylvia Lesombre, Ger MacEvilly, Una Mannion, Magella McGowan, Therese McGowan, Aine McGuire, Fabrice Niediu, Therese O'Loughlin, Sandra O'Malley, Joanna Pavlosky, Karen Stewart.

I would like to mention Oldways Preservation and Exchange Trust of Cambridge Massachusetts for inviting me to participate at their International Congresses. The encouragement you give to the local and traditional in support of good clean food is legendary and you have educated me and inspired me in my own small efforts. In particular I thank K. Dun Gifford and Sara Baer-Sinnott.

To John and Sally McKenna, who were the first people to write about Truffles, and the first critics in Ireland to concentrate on food first, rather than chintz.

Every town should have a Tir na nOg, a Kate's Kitchen and a Cosgroves. Sligo's great big larders.

The people who delivered, David, Gerry, Niall, Francis, Tina, Rod, Hans and Gaby, Colleen and the staff's heartthrob, Christie.

To those who have featured Truffles, confirming our convictions about food: Georgina Campbell, Petra Carter, Tom Doorley, Maureen Tatlow. Susan Stuck of Eating Well, Susan Lord and Danillo Baroncini from Gambero Rossa, Elisabeth Luard, Elle, John Whitley, Brian Waddell, Paul and Jeanne Rankin, Shauna from Bon Voyage, Clare McKeon. Suzanne Hamlin, who first introduced me to Oldways, a thousand thanks. Moira Hodgson, for her tremendous support, Karen Kaplan from Bon Appetit.

Sally McKenna, my editor, I would never have continued without you. I am deeply grateful.

Moya Homburger, Barry Guy for the title inspiration.

Those who tasted pizza at home: Inga Lloyd, Rod Alston, Tina, Elaine, Dolores Keegan, The Maloney-Lynch family, The Gunne's, and all my family.

Photo production was greatly assisted by Traditional Cheese, Frank Melvin, Noel Carter, Mary McDonnell, Kate Pettit, Rod and Tina from Eden Plants, Toby Simmonds, Jeffa Gill, Sally Barnes' Woodcock Smokery, Hans and Gaby Wieland.

Book production was greatly assisted by Joanna and Mathew Pavlosky, Gerry Byrne, Max Harvey, Ray Buckley, Erik Ryan, Pat Young, Eddie, and Leanna McMichael.

CONTENTS

FOREWORD

by John McKenna

Bernadette O'Shea's work has been of vital importance to the creation of a contemporary food culture in Ireland.

More than perhaps any other cook, Ms O'Shea hit upon the radical, the truly radical, idea of re-inventing an established culinary form – the pizza and its honourable flat-bread companions – and exploring how it could be reinterpreted to reflect not just the skills of a dazzlingly talented cook, but could also be used as a reflection of a local food culture, which produced uniquely fine foods. She brought the international back home to the local, and in this synthesis she created something utterly magical.

In this sense, what Bernadette O'Shea did in her work at **Truffles** restaurant, and in her intellectual re-imagining of what pizza can include and can accomplish, was to move beyond the idea of a culinary canon and to invent her own milieu. In Truffles, she was not merely director of a kitchen, she made herself – to borrow a cinematic term – an auteur; the pizzas did not merely explain themselves, they explained simultaneously their history and provenance, the concerns and obsessions of their inventor, and also the local food culture which inspired and directed them.

Bernadette O'Shea was uniquely fortunate to work with the produce of **Rod Alston, of Eden Herbs,** the finest grower in Ireland, and she assembled a team of dedicated, funky people to work with her.

The result – the pizzas, the focaccia, the calzone, the salads, the foods which are the content of this book, PIZZA DEFINED – were simply unforgettable.

The cooking demonstrated extraordinary grace, subtlety, extraordinary spirit, and yet there was nothing self-conscious about what the Truffles team did. They simply did what they wanted to do, in the way they wanted to do it. An obvious aspiration, perhaps, but in an Irish context, this was wild and radical behaviour. For their extremism, they succeeded on a scale almost beyond imagining.

When I first saw Bernadette O'Shea at work, her sense of rhythm and her instinctual ability to read the fluencies of diverse flavours put me in mind of a musician. The food in this book, the techniques which inform it and the sensibility which underpins it, seem likewise to demand comparison with music making. When the rhythm of the skill is mastered, the fluency and delight of the food is assured, the integrity and organic completeness of the combinations becomes utterly logical, harmonic, joyful.

PIZZA DEFINED is, in Irish terms, a radical book. But Bernadette O'Shea has already demonstrated her ability to conceive and to cope with the radical. In her hands, unorthodoxy becomes obvious, experimentalism discovers the logical. Her cooking is a definition of what cooking can be.

JOHN McKENNA

INTRODUCTION

Pizza belongs in the great tradition of flat breads, breads common to all cultures, Ireland included. Our own tradition of unleavened bread was always dependent on available ingredients. Seasonality was merely a necessity of existence, not the modern luxury we now need to work at to achieve. Breads made from scant ingredients, sometimes flour, always potatoes and salt, cooked originally over hot coals, were a quick and easy pick up food and more than often provided the only available daily nourishment.

As a child, lying one day under a travelling family's caravan, I remember seeing a woman grating potatoes against what looked like a coarse stone. The shredded potatoes were squeezed in her shawl, and mixed with flour and salt. This potato dough was rolled into thick sausages and cast onto a grate at the centre of hot glowing embers. I was given an end bit of a broken roll to eat and I've never forgotten the taste of the blackened ashy outer crust, the very flavour you will find on the bottom side of a pizza from a Neapolitan oven.

I have always loved working with and cooking bread, the outcome of a family life where my mother baked all our bread, cakes and puddings. The image of dough being kneaded is my foremost culinary memory, that and the memory of bread being baked, all around Templenoe in County Kerry, in cast iron casseroles over an open fire, with glowing hot coals placed on the lid to maintain an oven temperature. In essence every cook is formed at a young age, and the elements that I have loved from eating in my childhood – fresh breads, poached wild river salmon, fresh fish, cockles and mussels picked at the bottom of our land, my father's vegetables, all naturally grown and eaten in season, meat from our own stock, black pudding, my grandmother's great pears, my mother's great palate – encouraging new tastes – these are the elements which have come to dominate my cooking. There are cooks on both sides of my family, so the transition from teaching – my original career – to cooking professionally was perhaps inevitable.

I went to New York with the intention of getting as much culinary education as possible. My brother James of the West Street Grill, Litchfield, Connecticut, played a vital role in my re-education. He has taught me most about the gift of the palate, its boundaries, and its limitless possibilities. New York proved to be a wonderful window through which I saw incredible imagination at work when it came to pairing ingredients. This gave me even more enthusiasm for the quality of ingredients we had in Ireland.

I had a vague idea before going to New York that I wished to master the art of baking a pizza – it was certainly an appendage to the business of being a real cook! James introduced me to Evelyn Slomon, who was making great pizza at a restaurant in the Upper East Side. It was Evelyn who gave me my first ever pizza lessons, and I'm still grateful.

I kept many irons in the fire at that time and one of them was an opportunity to work for Patrick Clarke at Metro – it was chic, hot and new and had one of the best larders in New York, where expensive, incredible ingredients poured into the kitchen. At Evelyn's I discovered the very same ingredients were supplied to her restaurant and "all for a pizza?"

From this moment on, pizza for me, was elevated to new heights amongst the world's finest foods.

When I came back to Ireland I knew I wanted to work with pizza. I came to Sligo by default, explored the region and, finding an abundance of good ingredients around me, I stayed.

Truffles Restaurant started very simply – in fact, we literally closed on the first day as the furniture failed to arrive! – introducing Sligo to the great flavours of the Mediterranean: sun-dried tomatoes, olive oil, roast garlic, baked aubergines, Parmigiano Reggiano. Some of these ingredients had never been heard of in Ireland before, but Sligo people love new flavours, and gradually came to Truffles in droves.

But if Truffles introduced the people of Sligo to the tastes of the Mediterranean, Sligo became for me a vital source of the new artisan foods, the farmhouse cheeses, the organic vegetables, the hand-gathered seaweeds, the remarkable fish and shellfish, and my pizzas were a reflection of these ingredients. To have such a wealth of incredible produce to hand proved to be a restaurateur's dream.

The next big challenge in Truffles had to do with a commitment I made very early on to support organic produce. I discovered the work of Eden Plants, one of the finest organic gardens in the country. Once you work with clean food, produced without chemicals, there is no going back. The reasons are simple. The pure flavours of the ingredients help you to question the logic and the symmetries of food and cooking, and to explore what works together. The unparalleled texture is equally important. The seasonality, prized for surprise, and expectation, the excitement of the food calendar becoming an absorbing fascination. The sound nutritional values. Finally, it is the relationship between you and the earth, between you and the grower, between you and your care and responsibility for what your customers eat, between you and the shopkeeper who can provide the produce enjoyed at the restaurant. Above all else, it is about co-operation between people, it is about taking the mystery out of food, unlocking the fear people have in being accountable for our ingredients, naming sources. It is now very difficult for me to understand why it is not a first principle of every culinary institute and of every chef's kitchen. The quality of the ingredients at Truffles were always about good relations, inspiring and challenging me to use my medium as a cook to mirror its essential nature.

If good quality produce challenged the medium, then pizza was the ultimate messenger. The great interpreter.

BERNADETTE O'SHEA
BALLINTOGHER, CO SLIGO, 1997

PIZZA DEFINED

The recipes in this book have evolved over seven-and-a-half wonderful years spent cooking beside a pizza oven in Sligo, years spent sourcing, testing, tasting and, finally, serving to customers from the locality and from around the world. The popularity of my pizzas and the constant questioning and requests for explanation has culminated in my parting with the knowledge I gained, and with the recipes which define the particular qualities of the pizzas made in Sligo. Hence, PIZZA DEFINED.

From the very beginning, I understood that a good dough offers endless possibilities, and allows one the play of ingredients, the fun of sourcing, the complexity of multifarious flavour combinations. Pizza, in its original flatbread form, has been around since the stone ages. It is the great nomadic food, which served as an edible plate for the Etruscans who settled mainly in the North of Italy. The Etruscans flavoured their dough with herbs and spices, and used it as part of a meal. Today, in northern Italy, focaccia is served in a similar fashion – never intended as a meal in itself but as a snack. In the south of Italy it was the Greeks, with their wonderful baking skills acquired from the master bakers the Egyptians, who first made pizza into a complete meal, baking it with herbs, spices and meat on top.

Columbus brought the tomatoes to Italy, which served as ornamental garden plants – "golden apples" – for over 200 years before the Neapolitans had the courage to use them. There are many restaurants in Naples today which simply serve a flatbread, baked with oregano, garlic and tomato.

In the context of this history, I have been working at the oven a very short time! However, I try to keep my eye on the past as I work, but I am also informed by the palate of today, and the period we live in. Every cook has a duty to the past and an equal duty to the future, so that the period we live in may be recorded and will identify us by what we eat – thus telling future generations of our life style. It would be so boring to eat only what our ancestors ate, and equally boring to emulate only the new trends. I am grateful to both past and present. Both give me something for the future, both have allowed me to play with pizza, and define its scope.

THE NOBLE PIZZA

Pizza, a simple food, has a complicated little network of activities – all very simple but demanding serious attention to detail and intense organisation and planning. Pizza making is a process which demands time, with considered preparation of ingredients and a commitment to good food, where only the best ingredients should be used. Many people are quite shocked to discover that it is as costly to prepare a perfect pizza as any meat or fish dish.

People give up making pizzas because they begin without a menu, so to speak. They fail to read the instructions for making the dough, or to adhere accurately to each stage. Unclear about the type of pizza combinations and flavours they want to use, the dreaded, last minute exhortation, "let's have a pizza!", means abusing the dough and simply dumping leftovers or "whatever is in the fridge" onto the pizza. My advice is forget it.

Frequently people confuse pizza with fast food and pizza parlours, believing it to be a food which demands scant attention and absolutely no respect in its preparation. Pizza has mistakenly been driven into this camp, but rightfully pizza is a noble food, one of the great soul foods belonging to the rich flat bread traditions of the world. When the network of activities is understood, pizza making is simply one of life's greatest pleasures.

GREAT PIZZA

There are several very important stages in the process of making a pizza, and whilst mastering the technique requires a little patience, it leads eventually to an invaluable skill. It is crucial to spend time informing oneself about the stages of dough making and to practice them as often as possible. To rush this process or skip a stage is unforgivable!

The stages include:

MAKING THE DOUGH
KNEADING IT
ALLOWING IT TO RISE
FORMING THE OUTER RIM
STRETCHING
ASSEMBLING
BAKING

THE INGREDIENTS

The ingredients are yeast, flour, water, oil, salt – what could be simpler! I always use fresh yeast, and it is worth making an effort to get it even if it means begging the baker. Alternatively, and as a last resort, use active dry baker's yeast. Avoid the "quick rise" variety which forces the dough to rise in half the time – you also lose half the flavour and texture. Yeast causes the dough to rise as it lets out carbon dioxide and raises the tiny gluten cell structure in the dough. I instruct you to "stir in one direction", in order to avoid breaking up those tiny little cells which give a chewy, crusty, interior. Accuracy in maintaining the temperature of the water and the amount specified must be critically attended to. If you are unclear about the term "luke warm", then buy a thermometer.

We are very particular in this country about the water we use for our tea. It is just as important to use great water when making pizza dough. Avoid using hard, chlorinated or distilled water. Good spring water from the well is best of all. Alternatively use bottled spring water.

KNEADING

The dough is kneaded to develop the gluten in the flour – to develop elasticity and strength in the dough. It is impossible to over knead unless you use a food processor or electric mixer. It is generally impossible to work with overdeveloped gluten, so I would always advise hand kneading the dough.

On damp days a little extra flour might be required or a little less on a dry day. If you find the dough a little wet and hard to

handle, avoid adding the extra flour directly into the dough. Instead rub clean your hands and dust them with flour, and also dust the work surface with flour. Kneading will reduce this stickiness. When kneading, you are looking for a smooth elastic surface, if it is sticky then you have to knead a little more. Stickiness is not a problem, perseverance is!
Knead for the amount of time specified in the recipe.

PROVING

Whoever first instructed people to put the dough in the hot press or the airing cupboard has a lot to answer for. No two people's airing cupboards have the same temperature.

AVOID PROVING THE DOUGH IN THE AIRING CUPBOARD

A good draught free spot, away from an open door or window, is best. Make sure the cling film thoroughly seals the bowl. When the dough has doubled in bulk, it must be punched down straight away or it will collapse.

FORMING THE OUTER RIM

The rim is the outer, raised, edge of the pizza. This rim is formed before the pizza is stretched to its desired size. The rim has a number of functions. Firstly it prevents the sauce and the toppings from flowing onto the oven floor, called a pizza slide. It offers a textured difference, being drier and more crusty, and is a wonderful contrast to the richness of the gathered flavours in the centre of the pizza. As in nomadic days, it is like a handy or edible plate whereby one can lift the pizza from the dish and eat the food from one's hand without being scalded by the hot ingredients.
Take note of how the balls of dough are picked up, before forming the pizza. It is carefully done in this way in order to avoid touching the outer edge. Keeping this outer edge in perfect shape is crucial as it determines the appearance and shape of the pizza. When the pizza is first rolled by hand into a ball, it is at this point that a type of cast is formed which determines a definite circular shape to the pizza. Creating a perfect circle is not important, any shape is as good as another, but what makes a good pizza is the rim, regardless of the overall shape. So picking up the dough properly from the very beginning is actually part of forming a good rim.

STRETCHING

Avoid using a rolling pin – if you use a rolling pin you lose the rim of the pizza altogether and you lose texture, making the crust less chewy and too biscuit like.
Practice will make perfect. There are a few golden rules. Keep your hands well dusted with flour. To patch the torn dough do not use flour – simply pinch it together. Don't be tempted to tear off a piece and stick it on like a patch, you are not working with pastry! Deal with a tear straight away. Stretch evenly all around. Don't be

disturbed by the shape. Always avoid the rim when stretching. Never stretch the dough from the centre. If you stretch from the centre you will weaken the dough and it will be unable to take weighty ingredients and will definitely leak during cooking.

ASSEMBLING

Timing is everything. If I were with you I would say "hurry up" as every second passes. Check that the stretched pizza is sitting on a lightly floured surface and that the pizza peel is nearby and also lightly floured. Before stretching, all the ingredients should be lined up in order of use. I build each pizza carefully balancing ingredients – if a pizza is poorly constructed bits of ingredients will roll off when it is being placed in the oven and the overall appearance when cooked may look a mess. Follow my assembly patterns and later experiment with your own. The ideal assembly time is 1 minute!
The key to good assembly is organisation – be very organised.
I would actually mime this activity over an empty 20cm (8") plate, the saucing, assembling the other ingredients. I'd lift the plate onto the peel, and place it in the oven, and I'd time the mime!

THE PIZZA PEEL

A peel is a utensil designed to slide easily under the pizza and then slip the pizza into the oven. Practice using it with a stretched pizza dough before you assemble a full pizza. If you haven't got a peel, then use a rimless, flat baking tray. Ideally a short handled wooden pizza peel is best. Alternatively use a metal peel with a wood-en handle. Make sure you know the width of your oven before buying a peel.

BAKING

If you want to re-create the idea of an authentic pizza oven at home, then measure the bottom of the oven and buy unglazed terracotta tiles to cover the space. The tiles retain intense heat, unlike a baking tray. Make sure to place the tile in a cool oven – it will break if you place it in a hot oven, and always allow it to cool in the oven before you take it out.
Always preheat the oven an hour before you begin. Maximum intense heat is crucial to the formation of a good crust. Every oven has its faults, new or old. Generally the pizzas cook in about 10 minutes. With the first pizza check after 8 minutes to see if it is cooked. If the oven cooks unevenly rotate the pizza at this point. Gradually you will get used to the oven. Always bake the pizza on the bottom of the oven. The pizzas we photographed and all the recipes in the book were made in my home. I use a Smeg oven and I cook on manual. I found that the fan was unsuitable for pizza baking. Pizza depends on intense top and bottom heat, so fan assisted ovens are not the best.
When the pizza is cooked, remove from the oven and slice straight away. A pizza slicer is a good investment – it also slices more evenly and saves so much time

THE DOUGH

The ultimate and defining principle of great pizza is GREAT DOUGH

What I am trying to achieve with the dough is something which has its own great texture, its own flavour, and which also acts as an interpretive base for the rest of the ingredients. It should present an interesting contrast to the other softer juicier flavours that are baked with it.

So, I would look for a base which is a little chewy on the inside, crisp on the outside and firm enough to hold the ingredients up if you hold it by the rim. Obviously, if the ingredients on top are quite heavy this is impossible to do, but, the crust must always be crisp.

The pizza dough recipe I crafted in my home to match the dough I made at the restaurant. I think the base and the fine organic ingredients working together make a statement and what they say is

"THIS IS WHAT THIS FLATBREAD IS ABOUT, IT'S ABOUT A TRADITION OF GOOD FOOD. IT'S ABOUT A TRADITION OF INTERPRETING FOOD WHICH WE HAVE AROUND US"

THE DOUGH THAT FOLLOWS, ONCE MASTERED, WILL WIDEN THE CULINARY SCOPE OF EVERY COOK. SO IT IS IMPERATIVE BEFORE YOU BEGIN THAT YOU **READ THROUGH THE METHOD FROM BEGINNING TO END** AND THEN ENJOY THE PROCESS...

BASIC PIZZA DOUGH INGREDIENTS

350ml (12fl oz, $1^{1}/_{2}$ cups) of lukewarm water (113°F, 45°C)
20g ($^{3}/_{4}$oz) fresh yeast or 1 tablespoon active dried yeast
560g (1lb 2 oz, $3^{3}/_{4}$ cups) strong white flour
$^{3}/_{4}$ teaspoon salt
$2^{1}/_{4}$ tablespoons olive oil
35g ($1^{1}/_{4}$oz, $^{1}/_{4}$ cup) extra flour for kneading

UTENSILS

measuring cups and spoons
1 large bowl to combine ingredients
1 large bowl for the pizza to rise
small bowl for extra flour
wooden spoon
clean work surface, lightly floured
small bowl for yeast and water
dough scraper
scales
pizza peel
pizza stone or tile
knife to cut dough
cling film
oven timer

BEFORE YOU START to make a dough first assemble your utensils and then decide on the pizza you would like to make and gather your ingredients.

PUT THE STONE OR TILE in place one hour before cooking, and then preheat the oven to its maximum temperature.

1. STARTING OFF

- Pour the water into a bowl, and crumble in the fresh yeast or sprinkle over the dried yeast.
- Stir, allowing the yeast to dissolve.
- In a large bowl combine the flour and salt. Make a well in the centre, pour in the yeast mixture and olive oil.
- With a wooden spoon stir vigorously in one direction, working to the outside of the bowl until all the flour has been incorporated and the dough is quite soft and sticky.
- Turn the dough on to a very lightly floured work surface. It is now ready for kneading.
- Allow plenty of space for kneading.
- Rub excess dough from your hands.

2. KNEADING

- Lightly flour your hands.
- Grasp the dough with both hands and push the dough away from you with the heels of your hands, stretching it right across the work counter.
- Double the dough back on itself (fold it back) pressing both ends together.
- Give the dough a quarter turn and continue the kneading process.
- Knead the dough for about 12 minutes.

KNEADING NOTES:

Lightly flour your hands each time they become sticky but avoid adding flour to the dough. The stickiness is alleviated by good kneading.

If the work surface becomes sticky use a dough scraper to clean it and then lightly flour the surface again.

It is important to knead for the entire 12 minutes.

The properly kneaded dough should be smooth, almost shiny, soft and springy. When you push the heel of your hand down into the dough and it comes back clean you know it is time to stop kneading.

3. RISING

- Very lightly oil the inside of a bowl, which should be large enough for the dough to double in bulk (it makes it much easier for the dough to slide up the bowl and quickens the rising time).
- Place the dough in the oiled bowl and lightly brush the dough with oil.
- Cover the bowl tightly with cling film.
- Place the dough in a draught free area of the room (75°F-85°F, 25°-30°C).
- It takes about 40 to 50 minutes to double in bulk.

4. PUNCHING DOWN

- Remove the cling film and, with a clenched fist, punch down the dough.
- Remove from the bowl, and knead for a couple of minutes.
- Using a knife to cut the dough, divide it into six 140g (5oz) pieces, and shape each piece into a ball.

Each 140g (5oz) ball of dough makes one 20cm (8" inch) pizza.

- Place the balls onto an oiled tray, oil each ball lightly and cover the tray with cling film.
- If you are not going to use them straight away, place in the fridge.
- Otherwise allow to rest for 10 minutes before stretching and assembling.

5. FORM THE OUTER RIM

Before you begin, you may find it useful to cut out a 20cm (8") disc of paper, as it gives an idea of the size and stretchability of this particular weight of dough.

■ Lift a ball of pizza dough by sliding two fingers under the dough, with thumb on top, and gently lift it up from the centre.

■ Flour the pizza dough back and front and place on the lightly floured surface.

■ Keep surface and fingers lightly floured and have the dough scraper at hand, which is used in the event of the dough sticking to the surface.

■ To form the outer rim of the pizza dough press the tops of your fingers into the dough 10mm (½") in from the edge.

■ Repeat all around the edge of the pizza. Throughout the rest of the process make sure this outer rim remains untouched.

■ Inside the rim flatten the pizza dough with the tips of your fingers.

■ Turn the dough over and repeat the process, making the outer rim and dimpling down the centre of the pizza.

6. STRETCH THE PIZZA

■ Scrape and lightly flour the work surface and hands.

■ Pick up the dough and slap it hard onto the work surface.

Repeat this action once or twice.

■ Drape the dough over the clenched fingers of both hands with the thumbs resting side by side inside the rim of the pizza.

■ Apply a little pressure with both thumbs and gently move the thumbs apart stretching the dough a few inches at a time.

■ Move the right thumb onto the left thumb position and begin again with both thumbs together and repeat the process working in an anti-clockwise direction if right handed and clockwise direction if left handed.

■ As the size of the pizza increases it may be partially draped on the work surface which helps to avoid holes forming in the dough.

■ Should a hole form in the dough simply pinch it together with flour free fingers.

■ The stretching process really takes place just inside the rim of the pizza. Stretching from the centre would weaken the dough and cause holes to form during cooking.

THE DOUGH MUST BE EVEN ALL AROUND SO IT IS IMPERATIVE TO REMEMBER THE STARTING POINT WHEN STRETCHING.

When you have arrived back at the start, place the pizza on the work surface and examine it for evenness. On a first attempt the shape of the pizza is not a major consideration but it can still be manipulated into the destined shape when gently pressed and fingered on the work surface.

■ If at any time you are aware of a transparency in the dough or a small hole, the secret is to deal with it straight away. It is very unforgiving and will develop into a grand mess if it is not secured immediately.

7. ASSEMBLING THE PIZZA & USING THE PIZZA PEEL

■ Flour the pizza peel and leave it to one side until the pizza is ready to be placed in the oven.
■ Place the stretched pizza dough on a lightly floured surface.

AT THIS POINT ONE IS WATCHING THE CLOCK, AND INGREDIENTS SHOULD ALL BE LINED UP IN ORDER OF USE

■ Use both hands to spread the ingredients on the pizza.
■ With the sauce, it is imperative to spread it gently with the spoon barely touching the surface. The Mozzarella should be placed on the sauce at the opposite end of the pizza from you. Then with both hands comb it quickly over the sauce.
■ Add the remaining ingredients as instructed.
■ To slide the pizza onto the pizza peel hold the peel with one hand and very gently with the other hand lift up the outer lip of the pizza and in one quick movement slide the peel underneath.
■ Should the peel fail to slide all the way underneath simply jerk the peel back a little with your wrist and gently draw the pizza onto the peel with a brisk final jerk. It is really a wrist movement.
■ People are often tempted to keep pushing the peel forward. After you first slide in the peel the next movement is to jerk the peel back towards you, and bring the pizza in its momentum onto the peel.
■ If you find yourself pushing the pizza and peel forward you will cut into the pizza dough and cause it to leak when cooking.
■ If you get stuck simply slide the peel out from under the pizza and read the instructions again.

YES, IT TAKES PRACTICE

AND I WOULD ADVISE YOU TO PRACTICE THIS WITH A STRETCHED PIZZA BARE OF ALL INGREDIENTS...

PERHAPS YOUR FIRST PIZZA SHOULD BE ONE BAKED BLIND (SEE PAGE 102)

8. BAKING THE PIZZA

■ Open the oven door with one hand and with the other place the peel at the very back of the pizza tile, dropping its front rim onto the tile.
■ Gently jerk the pizza onto the tile and very quickly pull the peel away from under the pizza.
■ Quickly close the oven door.
■ Bake for approximately 8 minutes and then check the pizza. If you notice the crust a little darker on one side swivel the pizza around. Cook for approximately another 2 minutes.
■ The pizza is cooked when the crust is golden and crisp on the bottom – pick one edge up and tap it.
■ At the specified temperature the ingredients should also be cooked.

FOOD PROCESSOR METHOD

This is a method that I never use myself, either in the restaurant or at home. But it does work, so I am including it.

METHOD Put the warm water into the bowl, sprinkle on the yeast.

■ Pulse once or twice to dissolve the yeast.

■ Add flour, salt and oil and process until it forms a ball.

■ Knead to combine the dough. It takes only a few seconds – further kneading is not required.

ASSEMBLING THE PIZZA ON THE PEEL

This method, where a pizza is firstly placed on the peel and dressed whilst lying on it, may appear more simple, but because extra flour is used to prevent the dough from sticking to the peel, this flour becomes caked to the base of the pizza, causing it to blacken when placed in the oven.
This method also demands super speed, making it impossible to give as much care to the arrangement of ingredients on the pizza. It helps if one has a wooden peel, as the dough is less likely to stick to wood.

METHOD First flour the pizza peel and place the stretched dough on top.

■ Very quickly spread the sauce and all the other ingredients on the pizza making sure not to pile too much on it, as it will place pressure on the dough, causing it to stick to the peel and making it impossible to place in the oven.

■ Give the pizza peel a few jerks as you work to make sure the pizza still slides free before you place it in the oven.

■ If it has stuck, gently lift the sticky section up and place a little flour underneath and jerk the pizza up again to make sure it's free.

■ This is an acceptable method for pizzas baked blind and all the pizzas which carry very light ingredients.

SPONGE METHOD PIZZA DOUGH

This gives a kick start to the dough and is very simply made from a small quantity of the total ingredients of the dough. Yeast is dissolved in warm water and a little flour added and mixed to a loose batter. The longer it rests the better, as it greatly improves the texture and overall flavour of the dough. When making focaccia always use this method, rather than the basic pizza dough method.

INGREDIENTS FOR SPONGE METHOD

350ml (12fl oz, 1$\frac{1}{2}$ cups) lukewarm water
20g ($\frac{3}{4}$oz) fresh yeast or 1 tablespoon dried yeast
560g (1lb 2oz, 3$\frac{3}{4}$ cups) strong white flour
$\frac{3}{4}$ teaspoon salt
50ml (2fl oz, $\frac{1}{4}$ cup) olive oil

METHOD Pour 175mls (6fl oz, $\frac{3}{4}$ cup) of the warm water into a bowl which must be large enough to hold the dough when doubled in bulk.

■ Add the yeast and stir to dissolve.

■ Add 150g (5oz, 1cup) of flour and stir vigorously in the one direction until very well combined in a smooth batter.

■ Cover the bowl tightly with cling film and let it stand for a minimum of 25 mins, or up to 3 hrs, in a draught free area.

■ After rising remove the cling film, sprinkle on the salt, pour over the oil, a further 175ml (6fl oz, $\frac{3}{4}$ cup) of luke warm water and gradually add the final 410g (13oz, 2 $\frac{3}{4}$ cups) flour in a folding motion until completely incorporated.

■ Knead.

■ Place in an oiled bowl and brush the dough with oil.

■ Cover with a damp cloth.

■ Allow about two hours to double in bulk. Punch down.

POTATO & ROSEMARY FOCACCIA DOUGH

To make this focaccia dough I combine spelt with durum flour and blended wheat. Ideally I would use durum wheat on its own because it produces a wonderful rustic granular texture. The combination of spelt, durum and potatoes produces quite a dense focaccia with a rich wheaty flavour, but the bread is amazingly soft and light in spite of its density.

INGREDIENTS

225g (8oz, 1 packed cup) cooked potatoes
1 egg yolk
1/2 teaspoon salt
50ml (2fl oz, 1/4 cup) milk
2 tablespoons rosemary oil
225ml (8fl oz, 1 cup) warm water
20g (3/4oz) fresh yeast or 1 tablespoon active dried yeast
225g (8oz, 1 3/4 cups) durum flour with blended wheat
250g (9oz, 2 cups) spelt
3/4 teaspoon salt

METHOD

PEEL, COOK & DRAIN THE POTATOES
■ Add egg yolk, 1/2 teaspoon salt, milk, 1 tablespoon rosemary oil and mash.
■ Pour the warm water into another bowl, sprinkle over the yeast and stir to dissolve.
■ In a large bowl combine the flour with 3/4 teaspoon salt and half of the potatoes.
■ Make a well in the centre and pour in the yeast mixture and remaining oil.
■ Mix with a wooden spoon so that the ingredients combine well together.
■ Add in the remainder of the potatoes.
■ Should the dough appear to be a little dry when combining simply continue to mix (additional water will make it impossible to knead).
■ Turn out onto a lightly floured board and knead for 10 mins. It is quite a sticky dough, so keep the dough scraper at hand and continue to lightly flour your hands and work surface. Do not add flour directly to the dough.
■ Place the kneaded dough into a large, lightly oiled bowl and cover with cling film.
■ Place in draught free area for about 1 1/2 hours.
■ Punch down and use for Focaccia.

WHOLEMEAL PIZZA BASE

This base has a strong healthy wholesome flavour. It demands richer toppings than the white flour base as wholemeal has such a distinctive, assertive, texture and taste. It must generally be used with strong flavours – herbs, robust sauces, smoked meats etc.
Note: It is much stickier to work with than white flour dough.
Rosemary or lemon thyme are kneaded into this dough, and this technique can be used to flavour all doughs – chopped sundried tomatoes, herbs, chillis, fennel seeds or capers are all good when added to the basic pizza dough.

INGREDIENTS

200g (7oz, 1 1/4 cups) organic wholemeal flour
75g (2 1/2oz, 1/2 cup) potato flour
20g (3/4oz) fresh yeast or 1 tablespoon dried yeast
225mls (8fl oz, 1 cup) luke warm water
150g (5oz, 1 cup) organic white flour for kneading
1/4 teaspoon salt 2 tablespoons olive oil
1 tablespoon fresh rosemary, or lemon thyme leaves very finely minced

METHOD

COMBINE THE WHOLEMEAL FLOUR
and potato flour in a bowl.
■ Sprinkle the yeast over the warm water in another bowl and stir to dissolve.
■ Make a well in the centre of the wholemeal/potato flour and add the yeast mixture with the salt and oil.
■ With a wooden spoon stir vigorously in one direction until all the flour has been incorporated.
■ The dough should be quite sticky.
■ In the bowl, knead in the measured white flour and the herbs. Turn onto the work surface.
■ Knead for about 10 mins.

1. OPPOSITE: KNEADING

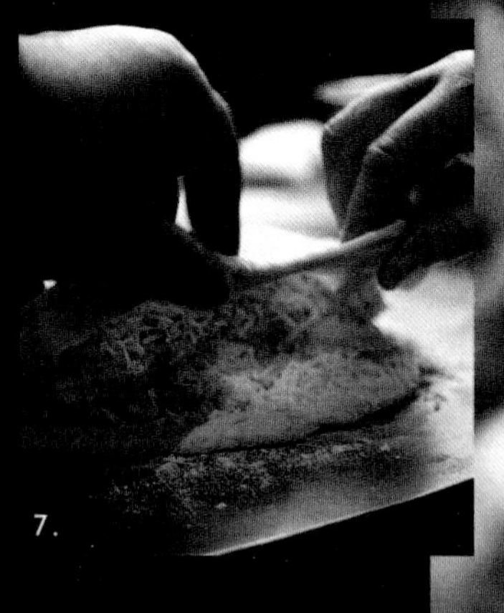

2. THE KNEADED DOUGH
3.DOUGH: BEFORE & AFTER RISING
4. FORMING THE OUTER RIM
5. SLAPPING THE DOUGH ONTO TABLE
6. STRETCHING THE DOUGH
7. FORMING A CALZONE
8. SLIDING THE PIZZA ONTO THE PEEL

8.

THE SAUCE

THE SAUCE IS ALWAYS SIMPLE

...SIMPLE FLAVOURS, SIMPLE INGREDIENTS

TOMATO, A LITTLE BIT OF GARLIC, BASIL AND OIL,

THAT'S IT

It's a total and natural complement to the pizza dough. The sauce is about creating moisture on a pizza, but it must be a complement both to the base and to the ingredients that are on top, and it should also work to intensify flavours.

It must never overstate its case, the sauce is there only as a flavour enhancer, it doesn't have the same status as the base or the other ingredients, it's there to give moisture, and there must only be enough: a couple of tablespoons.

Some ingredients need a stronger flavour, so use oven roasted tomatoes; smoked tomatoes; tomato and fennel to complement shellfish; ginger and tomato, which can also be served as a salsa.

If it doesn't have a major role, it does have an important role. You should hardly be aware of the sauce, but if it wasn't there you would miss it.

BASIC TOMATO SAUCE RECIPE

2 400g tins (1lb 12oz) plum tomatoes
olive oil
4 garlic cloves, thinly sliced lengthways
fresh black pepper (about 10 twists of the mill)
parmesan rind (optional)
10 basil leaves torn

■ Seed and break up the tomatoes (see right).
■ Heat a little olive oil over moderate setting.
■ Add the garlic and sauté until just tender.
■ Add the tomatoes, pepper and cheese rind.
■ As soon as the sauce begins to bubble reduce the heat and simmer, uncovered, for about 20 minutes, until the sauce thickens.
■ Add the basil leaves five minutes before end.

TO SEED TOMATOES

1. Pour the contents of a tin of tomatoes into a sieve, resting over a bowl.
2. Root out the seeds with your fingers.
3. Squash each seeded tomato between your fingers and add to the bowl beneath. Repeat this process with each tomato, and finally push the remaining juice through the sieve.
4. Discard the seeds.

OVEN ROASTED TOMATO SAUCE

4 cloves garlic, very thinly sliced
2 tablespoons olive oil
12 oven roasted tomatoes (SEE P. 36)
a few sprigs of rosemary

METHOD

■ Sauté the garlic in the olive oil until soft.
■ Break the roasted tomatoes into the pot and add a few sprigs of rosemary.
■ Cook to reduce the sauce to a fairly thick consistency. Remove the rosemary.

TOMATO & FENNEL SAUCE

olive oil
3 shallots, chopped
1 teaspoon fennel seeds
2 cloves garlic, finely sliced
400g (14oz) can plum tomatoes, seeded
freshly ground black pepper

METHOD

■ In a saucepan combine together the olive oil, shallots, garlic and fennel seeds.
■ Sauté until the shallots are soft.
■ Add the tomatoes and when they begin to bubble turn the heat down and simmer for 25-30 minutes.
■ Season with a little freshly ground black pepper.

SMOKED TOMATO SAUCE

12 tomatoes
salt
5 cloves garlic, very thinly sliced
2 tablespoons olive oil

METHOD

■ Slice tomatoes in half and sprinkle with salt.
■ Place in the basket of a smoker. Smoke for 45 minutes following the manufacturer's instructions (all smokers are different).
■ To make the sauce: heat the oil, add the garlic and sauté.
■ Add the smoked tomatoes. Simmer to reduce the sauce to a fairly thick consistency.

GINGER & TOMATO SAUCE

350g (12oz) tomatoes, peeled and seeded (preferably home grown)
1 tablespoon ginger, finely chopped
3 shallots
1 teaspoon powdered dry mustard
a dash of tabasco
1 teaspoon balsamic vinegar
1 teaspoon chives, chopped

METHOD

■ Puree tomatoes and shallots in a food processor to the desired texture (still slightly coarse).

■ Bring the tomato mixture to the boil and simmer gently, uncovered, for 10 minutes.
■ Stir in remaining ingredients.
■ Take off heat.
■ Serve as a sauce, or chilled as a relish.

Note:
This recipe can be used as a sauce on a pizza, or chilled and used as a relish.

GRILLED AUBERGINE PURÉE

1 large or 2 medium aubergines
1 tablespoon olive oil
1 tablespoon lemon juice
salt and freshly ground black pepper to taste

METHOD

■ Place aubergines directly under the grill and char/blacken the skin completely, turning frequently.
■ When still too hot to handle peel off the skin, discard any seeds and scoop the flesh into a bowl.
■ Add the oil and lemon juice.
■ Pound to a fine purée using a pestle and mortar.
■ Season with salt and black pepper.

Note:
The aubergines can also be split in half and baked in the top shelf in an extremely hot oven until cooked.
However, this doesn't have anything like the flavour of the grilled aubergine.

AUBERGINE SAUCE

2 aubergines
16 cloves of garlic
4 tablespoons olive oil
50mls (2fl oz, 1/4 cup) lemon juice
3 tablespoons balsamic vinegar
Salt and pepper to taste

METHOD

■ Split the aubergines in half, lengthways and place on a baking tray. Into the flesh of each half, press four cloves of garlic and dribble over a tablespoon of olive oil.
■ Bake in a hot oven for 20 minutes approximately, until both the garlic and the aubergine are soft.
■ Chop the cooked aubergine into chunks and place it all (including the skin) in a mortar with the lemon juice and vinegar.
■ Pound with a pestle to a smooth consistency, and season to taste.

ONION SAUCE

75ml (2 1/2fl oz, 1/3 cup) olive oil
900g (2lbs) onions, sliced
3 garlic cloves, minced
1 bay leaf
1/2 teaspoon freshly ground black pepper
1 tablespoon fresh thyme leaves or 2-3 sprigs fresh rosemary
1/4 teaspoon salt

METHOD

■ Heat the oil in a large saucepan over medium heat.
■ Add all the ingredients and stir to combine.
■ Gently simmer for about an hour, uncovered.
■ Check back and stir occasionally.
■ When the onions have caramelised and most of the moisture is gone remove from the heat.
■ When cool remove the bay leaf and rosemary sprigs.

HOT CHILLI SAUCE

olive oil
1 small onion, finely diced
1 dried or fresh red chilli
1/8 teaspoon of cayenne pepper
400g (14oz) can plum tomatoes, seeded

METHOD

■ Warm the olive oil in a saucepan.
■ Sauté the onion until almost golden.
■ Add in the chilli and cayenne pepper and continue to sauté for one more minute.
■ Stir in the tomatoes and cook, for about 15-20 minutes, until the sauce reduces and becomes quite thick.

BASICS

Many of the staple ingredients of the pizza come straight out of the Mediterranean tradition:

GARLIC, OLIVES, PEPPERS

they remind us of sunshine, of the healthy Mediterranean diet, generous, fabulous flavours.

We should also have great respect for what we grow ourselves.
We can put our mark on the map, the culinary map, by virtue of our ingredients.

ROAST GARLIC

2 or more heads garlic
4 teaspoons olive oil

- Preheat the oven to 240°C, 500°F, Gas 9.
- Put the separated but unpeeled cloves of garlic into a loaf pan.
- Toss in about 4 teaspoons of olive oil and roast for 20 mins.
- Half way through toss the garlic to check it isn't browning too quickly.
- The garlic is ready when it is just tender.

TO ROAST A HEAD OF GARLIC

- Preheat the oven to 240°C, 500°F, Gas 9.
- Slice the top off the whole head of garlic and place the base on a baking tray with the cut tips facing upwards.
- Drizzle with olive oil and roast for approx. 20 mins.
- Serve as an anti-pasta.
- It makes a great centrepiece to the dinner table.
- Scoop out the cloves and use to smear on bread or focaccia.

CARAMELISED GARLIC

200g (7oz, $1\frac{1}{2}$ cups) peeled garlic cloves
300mls ($\frac{1}{2}$ pint, $1\frac{1}{4}$ cups) balsamic vinegar
3 teaspoons olive oil

- Cook all the ingredients in a saucepan, uncovered, over a moderate heat until the cloves are cooked and the vinegar is thick and syrupy.

GRILLED PEPPERS

6 peppers
olive oil

- Split the peppers in half lengthways and remove the seeds.
- Brush the skin with olive oil and place, skin side up, under a hot grill.
- It takes about 10 minutes to completely blacken/char the skin.
- Remove from the grill and place in a bowl.
- Cover the bowl tightly with cling film.
- When cooler remove all the skin.

▪ You can also bake the half peppers in the top rack of a preheated 240°C, 500°F, Gas 9 oven.
▪ Bake for 10-15 minutes, until the peppers are tender, and the skin begins to blacken.

RATATOUILLE

olive oil
2 medium onions, diced
2 medium aubergines, diced
2 red peppers, diced
1 green pepper, diced
3 courgettes, diced
400g (14oz) can tomatoes, seeded
2 cloves garlic, chopped
salt and freshly ground black pepper
10 basil leaves

▪ Sauté the onions, aubergines, peppers and courgettes in a generous amount of olive oil for approximately 10 minutes.
▪ Add the tomatoes and then the garlic and cook for a further 10 minutes until it softens with the vegetables still distinct.
▪ Season and add basil five minutes before the end of cooking.

BAKED RED CABBAGE & RED ONION SALAD

250g (9oz, 1 very small) red cabbage, quartered and thinly sliced
140g (5oz, 1 large) red onion, quartered and thinly sliced
25g (1oz) fresh or pickled ginger, very finely chopped
1 tablespoon soya sauce
125ml (4fl oz, 1/2 cup) of balsamic vinegar
70g (2 1/2oz, 1/3 cup) sugar
5-6 twists freshly ground black pepper
1/2 teaspoon salt
50ml (2fl oz, 1/4 cup) olive oil

▪ Preheat the oven to 180°C, 350°F, Gas 4.
▪ Mix all the ingredients except the oil together and let stand for a few minutes.
▪ Warm the oil in an oven proof casserole.
▪ Add the red cabbage mixture, cover and bake in the oven for 40 mins.
▪ Give the occasional shake or stir to the casserole during cooking.
This Salad can be used in three different ways: either raw, hot from the oven, or allowed to cool to room temperature.

OVEN ROASTED TOMATOES

12 tomatoes, sliced in two
sea salt
50ml (2fl oz, 1/4 cup) olive oil
rosemary

- Preheat the oven to 90°C/180°F/Gas 1/4.
- Sprinkle tomatoes with salt and drizzle with olive oil and arrange small rosemary stalks on top.
- Place side by side on a wire rack over a baking dish in the oven.
- Bake for 12 hours. (NB This is ideal in the slow oven of an Aga).
- Alternatively, place in a preheated 130°C/250°F/Gas 1/2 oven for about 3 hours.
- The tomatoes will be a little firm with this second method, but they're still delicious.

OVEN ROASTED TOMATOES WITH BLACK PEPPER

12 tomatoes
50ml (2fl oz, 1/4 cup) olive oil
2 teaspoons coarse salt
2 cloves minced garlic
2 tablespoons freshly ground black pepper

- Preheat oven to 100°C/200°F/Gas 1/4.
- Slice the tomatoes in two and place on a baking tray.
- Combine the rest of the ingredients together and pack down on to the cut side of the tomatoes.
- Place the tray in the preheated oven and slowly bake for at least 8 to 12 hours.

OVEN-ROASTED CHERRY TOMATOES

16 Cherry Tomatoes
salt
olive oil

- Preheat oven to 100°C/200°F/Gas 1/4.
- Place the whole tomatoes on a wire rack, brush with olive oil and sprinkle with salt.
- Roast for three hours; five hours if you want a more intense flavour.

OPPOSITE: OVEN-ROASTED TOMATOES

GRISSINI

To make these BREAD STICKS, preheat the oven to 240°C, 500°F, Gas 9.
Pull off a little basic pizza dough and roll it between your fingers.
Place on the counter and continue to shape into irregular, finger thin bread sticks.
Wet your fingers and dampen the dough, then sprinkle on salt, or chopped garlic, salami, sesame seeds or fennel seeds.
Place on a large preheated baking tray or pizza tile and bake until golden brown. Grissini must have a good hard crunch.

TAPENADE

175g (6oz, 1 cup) black olives, pitted
2 tablespoons capers
2 cloves garlic, minced
3 tablespoons olive oil
3 tablespoons lemon juice
2 anchovies

Pound all the ingredients together using a pestle and mortar until you reach the desired texture, which can be chunky or smooth.

GREEN OLIVE TAPENADE

115g (4oz) green olives
3 anchovy fillets
2 cloves garlic
1 tablespoon olive oil
black pepper to taste

Pound together using a pestle and mortar to desired consistency.

BALSAMIC VINAIGRETTE

75ml (2½fl oz, ⅓ cup) good quality aged balsamic vinegar
225ml (8fl oz, 1 cup) pure olive oil
1 teaspoon freshly ground black pepper
1-2 teaspoons salt
2 teaspoons Dijon mustard
2 level teaspoons minced garlic

Put the ingredients in a jar and shake well.
Alternatively you can use basil oil, in which case leave out mustard and garlic.

OPPOSITE: GRISSINI

ROASTED PEPPER & ALMOND SAUCE

2 large red peppers, grilled and peeled (SEE P. 35)
150g (5oz, 1 cup) almonds, blanched
1 clove garlic, minced
1 tablespoon parsley, finely chopped
salt and freshly ground black pepper
50mls (2fl oz, 1/4 cup) balsamic vinegar
100mls (4fl oz, 1/2 cup) olive oil

- Roast the almonds in a hot (425°F, 220°C, Gas 7) oven for about 5 mins, until just brown – watch carefully, they burn easily – and then place in a food processor and process until roughly ground.
- Using a pestle and mortar pound the peppers until a smooth texture is achieved.
- Add the remaining ingredients, except the olive oil.
- Pound again, while gradually streaming in the olive oil to combine.

HOMEMADE PESTO

140g (5oz) fresh basil leaves
55g (2oz) fresh mint leaves
115g (4oz) pine nuts
70g (2 1/2oz) Parmesan, freshly grated
225ml (8fl oz, 1 cup) or more of extra virgin olive oil depending on the consistency you need

- Combine the basil, mint, nuts and parmesan together and, using a pestle and mortar grind to a paste while slowly adding the olive oil.

NOTE This can also be made in a food processor but it is worth the effort to do it by hand.

ONION CONFIT

85g (3oz) butter
3 onions peeled and thinly sliced
1 large teaspoon sugar
225mls (8fl oz, 1 cup) red wine
50mls (2 fl oz, 1/4 cup) sherry vinegar
1 tablespoon Cassis
50mls (2 fl oz, 1/4 cup) vegetable stock (optional)
salt and freshly ground black pepper
fresh thyme leaves

- Melt the butter in a heavy bottomed saucepan over a moderate heat.
- Add the onions, cover and cook for 10 minutes.
- Halfway through add the sugar, salt and pepper.
- Add the fresh thyme, wine, sherry vinegar and Cassi s. Give the pot a good stir and continue to cook for about 1 hour uncovered, over a low heat.

■ If at any stage the liquid should evaporate simply add a little more wine or vegetable stock.
■ Remove from the heat and place in a bowl, making sure to scrape out all the syrupy liquid.
■ When cool, cover and store in the fridge. It will hold for about a week.

TOMATO PESTO

115g (4oz) sun-dried tomatoes
4 anchovies (optional)
55g (2oz) walnuts, chopped
175mls (6fl oz, 3/4 cup) olive oil (more can be added if required)
1 1/2 dessertspoon Balsamic vinegar
Pinch cayenne pepper
1 heaped teaspoon garlic, finely chopped

■ Place the tomatoes, anchovies and walnuts in a mortar, and pound.
■ Add the oil gradually, followed by the vinegar, pepper, and finally the garlic.

ONION PURÉE

450g (1 lb) small onions
olive oil
225mls (8fl oz, 1 cup) vegetable stock
1 tablespoon chopped sage
1 bay leaf
zest of half a lemon
2 tablespoons sour cream

■ Brown the onions on top of the stove in a little olive oil.
■ Place in a baking tray with vegetable stock, sage and bay leaf and simmer in a 400°F, 200°C, Gas 6 oven until the onions are tender. Purée.
■ Add the lemon zest and the sour cream.

FAVA BEAN CREAM

500g (1lb 2oz) fava beans (broad beans), shelled
55g (2oz) butter
1 1/2 tablespoons fresh cream
salt and pepper

■ Cook the beans for about a minute in boiling salted water. Drain. Reserve 55g (2oz) of the cooked beans for the pizza.
■ Place the rest in a food processor with the other ingredients and process until smooth.

BABA GHANOUSH

2 aubergines
16 cloves of garlic
4 tablespoons olive oil
1½ tablespoons tahini
¾ teaspoon cayenne pepper (plus more if desired)

- Preheat the oven to 425°F, 220°C, Gas 7.
- Split the aubergines down the middle lengthways, press 4 cloves garlic into the flesh of each half and drizzle each half with 1 tablespoon olive oil.
- Bake for 30 minutes.
- Using a pestle and mortar pound the aubergines (including skin and garlic) together with the tahini and pepper until a desired consistency.
- Taste as you go along, the more you pound the more intense the flavour.
- Use as a dipping sauce for Grissini, in a Focaccia sandwich, or on pizza baked blind.

SOUR CREAM

450ml (16 fl oz, 2 cups) cream
5 teaspoons buttermilk

- Place 225ml (8fl oz, 1 cup) of cream in a jar with a sealed top.
- Add the buttermilk and shake well.
- Stir in the remaining cream and cover tightly.
- Store at a warm room temperature for 24 hours.
- The sour cream may be used now, but for best results store in the fridge for another 24 hours.
- The cream will keep for a week or more.

CRÈME FRAÎCHE

3 parts fresh cream to 1 part buttermilk
Both at room temperature

- Combine the cream and buttermilk and cover with cling film.
- Leave at room temperature for 12 hours.
- Remove thickened crème fraîche to glass jug with tight fitting lid and refrigerate.
- It will hold for about 6 days.

THE PIZZAS

VEGETABLE, HERB & CHEESE PIZZAS

RED CABBAGE WITH AUBERGINE

This pizza was created partly due to improvising with ingredients that were at hand, and partly by the fact that I had just gone on a diet, and decided to reduce all dairy produce. I gathered some ingredients together, popped them in the oven, and out came my baked cabbage.
I spread my sauce on the pizza, topped it with the red cabbage, and it was perfect.
I love the colour contrast between the aubergine purée and red cabbage, and the pistachio nuts on the top with that little shade of purple. I didn't want anything to take from the intensity of the cabbage, so the aubergine proved to be a perfect foil for those flavours.
I also thought it was a great vegan alternative.

INGREDIENTS

140g (5oz) basic pizza dough (SEE P. 17)
115g (4oz, 1/2 cup) of grilled aubergine purée (SEE P. 31)
225g (8oz, 1 cup) of casserole baked red cabbage and onion (SEE P. 35)
55g (2oz) pistachio nuts

METHOD

PLACE PIZZA TILE on floor of the oven and preheat to maximum for one hour.

ASSEMBLING THE PIZZA Stretch the dough into a 20cm (8") circle, spread the aubergine sauce over the pizza 10mm (1/2") in from the rim.

- Spread the red cabbage mixture in an even light layer over the purée.
- Scatter pistachio nuts on top.
- Bake in the preheated oven for approx. 10 mins.

Alternatively the base can be baked blind and ingredients – at room temperature – added as above. Or the base can be baked blind and then topped with the cabbage mixture – omit the aubergine sauce – and fresh figs. Both fresh prunes and fresh figs may be added to pizza when baked.

OPPOSITE: RED CABBAGE WITH AUBERGINE PIZZA. OVERLEAF: LEEK & GOAT'S CHEESE PIZZA (SEE P. 53)

BAKED AUBERGINE PIZZA

Aubergine can be very bland on its own, so you have to work with it. My preferred way is to grill aubergines, then put them into a pestle and mortar with herbs. After paying a visit to Istanbul where aubergines are traditionally char-grilled, I realised that this is particularly the best method. It needs that subtle burnt flavour, then it is wonderful.

INGREDIENTS

140g (5oz) basic pizza dough (SEE P. 17)
2 small aubergines
olive oil
2 tablespoons tomato sauce (SEE P. 30)
2 tablespoons aubergine sauce (SEE P. 31)
6 cloves garlic, roasted
6 anchovies
8 olives
1 clove garlic, very finely chopped
basil leaves

METHOD

PLACE PIZZA TILE on floor of the oven and preheat to maximum for one hour.

TO COOK THE AUBERGINE Thinly slice the aubergines, brush with olive oil back and front. Char grill until tender, or place in a single layer on a baking tray and bake in a hot oven, until lightly browned.

ASSEMBLING THE PIZZA Stretch the dough into a 20cm (8") circle, spread over the tomato sauce, 10mm (½") in from the rim.
- Arrange the aubergine slices on the sauce.
- In the middle of the pizza and on top of the slices, spoon on the aubergine sauce.
- Flatten with the back of a spoon.
- Arrange the roast garlic, anchovies and olives on the pizza.
- Sprinkle with the chopped garlic and bake in the preheated oven for approx. 10 mins.
- Serve with fresh basil leaves.

PESTO WITH AUBERGINE

This pizza arose purely out of having a bowl of pesto on the counter, and a glut of aubergines, and pairing the two together.
Perhaps one reason why this combination succeeds is because aubergine is another vegetable that simply adores mint, and so it echoes the mint I use in the pesto.
Over the years I began to add extra flavours, goat's cheese, and pine nuts. Pesto with Aubergine was one of the most popular pizzas in the restaurant.

INGREDIENTS

140g (5oz) basic pizza dough (SEE P. 17)
1 large or 2 small aubergines
olive oil
2 tablespoons pesto
140g (5oz) goat's cheese
25g (1 oz) pine nuts
55g (2oz) Parmesan, freshly grated
1 clove garlic, very finely chopped
Parmesan shavings & basil leaves

METHOD

PLACE PIZZA TILE on floor of the oven and preheat to maximum for one hour.

TO COOK THE AUBERGINE Chop into wedges. Toss in olive oil and bake in preheated oven until brown on both sides.

ASSEMBLING THE PIZZA Stretch the dough into a 20cm (8") circle, spread over the pesto, 10mm (½") in from the rim.
- Top with aubergine.
- Dot with goat's cheese.
- Sprinkle on pine nuts, Parmesan and fresh garlic.
- Bake for approx. 10 mins.
- Remove from oven – scatter over Parmesan and basil.

PREVIOUS PAGE: GRILLED PEPPER & ROAST GARLIC PIZZA (SEE P. 52). OPPOSITE: PESTO WITH AUBERGINE PIZZA

GRILLED PEPPERS & ROAST GARLIC

I first ate a combination like this cooked by Evelyn Slomon. When I came back home I created different variations, using the Parmigiano Reggiano, adding a good drizzle of basil oil, and the contrast of the salty ricotta worked wonderfully well with the mild, slightly chargrilled flavour of the peppers.
Grilled peppers and roast garlic was one of the first pizzas I put on the menu, and I called it Truffles Best.

INGREDIENTS

140g (5oz) basic pizza dough (SEE P. 17)
2 tablespoons basic tomato sauce (SEE P. 30)
70g (2½ oz) Mozzarella, grated
85g (3oz) Ricotta Salata, crumbled
10 cloves roast garlic, peeled (SEE P. 34)
2 small grilled peppers, torn into strips (SEE P. 35)
85g (3oz) Parmesan, freshly grated
1 clove garlic, very finely chopped
basil oil (SEE P.122) & fresh basil leaves

METHOD

PLACE PIZZA TILE on floor of the oven and preheat to maximum for one hour.

ASSEMBLING THE PIZZA Stretch the dough into an 20cm (8") circle, spread the tomato sauce over the pizza 10mm (½") in from the rim.
- Scatter the Mozzarella over the sauce.
- Crumble over the Ricotta.
- Then add the garlic cloves and arrange the grilled pepper strips on top, like the spokes of a bicycle wheel.
- Sprinkle on half of the Parmesan with the chopped garlic.
- Bake in the preheated oven for approx. 10 mins.
- Just before serving add the remaining Parmesan.
- Drizzle with the basil oil and arrange the basil leaves on top.

If you can't get ricotta salata use feta, and the peppers may be roasted, rather than grilled, in a 500°F, 240°C, Gas 9 oven until the skins are blackened. Remove and place in a bowl covered with cling film. Then use as grilled peppers.

LEEK & GOAT'S CHEESE

This is traditional, like the lovely little goat's cheese tarts with leeks which you might have in France.
Here I combine some of Sligo's goat's quark with St Tola goat's log. The two combine brilliantly together, and the only natural accompaniments are small slim, slender leeks and the woody flavour of thyme.

INGREDIENTS

140g (5oz) basic pizza dough (SEE P. 17)
175g (6oz) leeks, sliced
olive oil
2 small potatoes, thinly sliced
70g (2½ oz) goat's quark
115g (4oz) goat's cheese, crumbled
1 tablespoon fresh thyme leaves
salt and freshly ground black pepper
1 clove garlic, very finely chopped
rosemary oil (SEE P. 122)

METHOD

PLACE PIZZA TILE on floor of the oven and preheat to maximum for one hour.

TO COOK THE LEEKS Sauté leeks in a little olive oil until tender. Alternatively toss in a little olive oil, place on a baking tray and cook in a hot oven. When cooked, season with salt and pepper and a few drops of rosemary oil (optional). Allow to cool.

TO COOK THE POTATOES Warm a little oil and add the sliced potatoes, tossing well to combine with the oil. Sauté for about 5 mins. Season with salt, black pepper and thyme leaves. Incorporate these flavours very gently making sure to retain the shape of the sliced potatoes. Can be used warm.

ASSEMBLING THE PIZZA Stretch the dough into a 20cm (8") circle, spread the leeks over the pizza 10mm (½") in from the rim.

- Dot with the goat's quark and goat's cheese.
- Arrange the sliced potato on top avoiding overlapping.
- Sprinkle chopped garlic on top (optional).
- Bake in the preheated oven for approx. 10 mins.

If you can't find goat's quark use a very soft mild goat's cream cheese.

PEARL ONIONS, ANCHOVIES & OLIVES

A very simple pizza, slightly understated, but the intensity of the glazed pearl onions and the contrast of the anchovies is, I suppose, in a very different way, my reworking of the flavours of the south of France. Those beautiful white pearl onions, then the anchovies and olives just complementing each other. It's a pizza with woody flavours, intense and delicious.

INGREDIENTS

140g (5oz) basic pizza dough (SEE P. 17)
10 pearl onions
125ml (4 fl oz, 1/2 cup) good vegetable stock
2 1/2 tablespoons tomato and ginger sauce (SEE P.31)
8 green olives
5 anchovies
lemon rind, very finely slivered

METHOD

PLACE PIZZA TILE on floor of the oven and preheat to maximum for one hour.

TO GLAZE THE PEARL ONIONS Cook the onions with the stock in a hot, 500°F, 240°C, Gas 9, oven until they become tender and glazed. Cool.

ASSEMBLING THE PIZZA Stretch the dough into a 20cm (8") circle, spread the tomato and ginger sauce over the pizza 10mm (1/2") in from the rim.

- Spread over the onions.
- Arrange the olives and anchovies on top and bake in the preheated oven for approx. 10 mins.
- Serve garnished with lemon rind.

115g (4oz) goat's cheese may be added. If so, reduce the amount of sauce to 2 tablespoons. You can also add sautéed potatoes.

TOMATO AND AVOCADO PIZZA

A glut of tomatoes arrived on my table from Eden Plants. The most complementary foods are tomato and Parmesan and, as an interesting, soft contrast I added in the avocado.

It's a summertime, light, fun sort of pizza. It has to have lots of basil and fresh garlic on it, and this is a pizza which demands good tomatoes: home-grown, firm textured, sweet, with bulging fruit flavours.

INGREDIENTS

140g (5oz) basic pizza dough (SEE P. 17)
2 tablespoons basic tomato sauce (SEE P. 30)
2 ripe avocados, sliced
plum tomatoes or good quality home grown tomatoes, thinly sliced
fresh basil leaves
140g (5oz) Parmesan, freshly grated
1 clove garlic, very finely chopped
basil oil (optional) (SEE P.122)

METHOD

PLACE PIZZA TILE on floor of the oven and preheat to maximum for one hour.

ASSEMBLING THE PIZZA Stretch the dough into a 20cm (8") circle, spread the tomato sauce over the pizza 10mm (1/2") in from the rim.

- Arrange the sliced avocados on the pizza and top with the tomatoes making sure they do not overlap.
- Place a basil leaf under each slice of tomato.
- Sprinkle the Parmesan and garlic over the pizza.
- Bake in the preheated oven for approx. 10 mins.
- Drizzle basil oil on the cooked pizza. Serve with extra Parmesan and some pesto.

SPINACH WITH THREE CHEESES

Spinach is wonderful with cheeses, and whilst I love spinach, I almost selected it here simply for the colour. It gives a beautiful colour contrast on a pizza, and when I tried it for myself, I just thought, this works, it's just perfect, simply steam the spinach, add nothing. I used to add butter, but then I became aware of having a lot of dairy produce on this pizza, so I dropped the butter and I found it worked just as well.

INGREDIENTS

140g (5oz) basic pizza dough (SEE P. 17)
175g (6oz) cooked spinach, well drained
2 tablespoons basic tomato sauce (SEE P. 30)
70g (2½ oz) Mozzarella, grated
1-2 tomatoes, very thinly sliced
fresh basil leaves
115g (4oz) cream cheese, crumbled
1 clove garlic, very finely chopped
85g (3oz) Parmesan, freshly grated
shredded basil oil (see below)

METHOD

PLACE PIZZA TILE on floor of the oven and preheat to maximum for one hour.

SHREDDED BASIL OIL 6 hours ahead very finely shred a cup of basil leaves and add 450ml (16 fl oz, 2 cups) of olive oil. Leave to sit at room temperature.

TO COOK THE SPINACH
- Wash thoroughly in three changes of water.
- Shake off excess water.
- Place in a saucepan over a high heat.
- Cover, and when it begins to steam toss the spinach.
- Turn the heat down low and allow the spinach to cook until tender.
- Squeeze out excess water.

ASSEMBLING THE PIZZA Stretch the dough into a 20cm (8") circle, spread over the tomato sauce, 10mm (½") in from the rim.
- Scatter over the Mozzarella.
- Circle tomatoes around outer edge of the pizza maintaining your rim – do not overlap.
- Tuck basil leaves underneath.
- Place the spinach in the centre of the pizza.
- Dot the cream cheese on top.
- Sprinkle over the garlic and Parmesan, reserving just a little of the Parmesan to sprinkle on the pizza just before serving.
- Bake in the preheated oven for approx. 10 mins.
- Sprinkle on reserved Parmesan and drizzle a little of the basil flavoured oil and the shredded basil over the tomatoes and serve.

PISSALADIÈRE PIZZA

South of France, wild thyme-scented fields, as traditional as can be, and this is my interpretation of it. The sauce is the key: it has to have a lovely balance of moisture and a sweet onion reduction with the herbs. You already have enough salt with the anchovies, while pine nuts give a lovely, nutty crunch.

INGREDIENTS

140g (5oz) basic pizza dough (SEE P. 17)
175g (6oz, 3/4 cup) onion sauce (SEE P. 31)
55g (2oz) pine nuts
8 anchovies
10 olives
1 teaspoon thyme leaves

METHOD

PLACE PIZZA TILE on floor of the oven and preheat to maximum for one hour.

ASSEMBLING THE PIZZA

Stretch the dough into a 20cm (8") circle, spread the onion sauce over the pizza 10mm (1/2") in from the rim.
- Arrange the olives and anchovies on top.
- Scatter over the pine nuts and sprinkle on the thyme leaves.
- Bake in the preheated oven for approx. 10 mins.

PESTO PIZZA

I met Emanuella Stucci in Puglia, and we were walking in for lunch together and I could smell the brushcetta inside, the char-grilling, the tomatoes, the basil and it made me think of pesto. I said that I often made bruschetta at home and put pesto on it, and she said, "Yes, we put a little mint in our pesto." She said it makes it less sharp, a bit sweeter, so as soon as I went home, straight away, the first thing I tried was mint in my pesto, and I haven't looked back since. I never make pesto without mint now. It's divine on pizza, completely wonderful.

INGREDIENTS

140g (5oz) basic pizza dough (SEE P. 17)
2 tablespoons tomato sauce (SEE P. 30) (optional)
70g (2 1/2 oz) Mozzarella, grated
55g (2oz) cream cheese
1 tablespoon home made pesto (SEE P. 40)
8 anchovies
10 olives
1 clove garlic, very finely chopped
25g (1oz) Parmesan, freshly grated
fresh basil leaves

METHOD

PLACE PIZZA TILE on floor of the oven and preheat to maximum for one hour.

ASSEMBLING THE PIZZA

Stretch the dough into a 20cm (8") circle.
- Spread the tomato sauce over the pizza 10mm (1/2") in from the rim.
- Distribute the Mozzarella evenly over and dot with the cream cheese leaving the centre free.
- Spread the pesto in the centre.
- Arrange the anchovies and olives on top and sprinkle with chopped garlic.
- Bake in the preheated oven for approx. 10 mins.
- A few mins before the end of cooking time add the Parmesan.
- Garnish with the basil.

CALIFORNIA CLASSIC

This pizza is all about my idea of California, the flavours of the sun. If you think of the new wave of Californian cuisine, this is the sort of thing they would have begun with, I'm sure. I thought, oh, I could bring that home and bottle it and put it on a pizza. This was one of the first pizzas I made and it was very experimental in that people would never have had these flavours together on a pizza. So this was what I called a new age pizza, the new interpretations of great food for our times.

INGREDIENTS

140g (5oz) basic pizza dough (SEE P. 17)
2 tablespoons basic tomato sauce (SEE P. 30)
85g (3oz) Mozzarella, grated
55g (2oz) sun-dried tomatoes, torn into strips
140g (5oz) goat's cheese, crumbled
10 cloves roast garlic (SEE P. 34)
55g (2oz) Parmesan, freshly grated
1 clove garlic, very finely chopped (optional)
Fresh basil leaves
basil oil (SEE P.122)

METHOD

PLACE PIZZA TILE on floor of the oven and preheat to maximum for one hour.

ASSEMBLING THE PIZZA Stretch the dough into a 20cm (8") circle, spread the tomato sauce over the pizza 10mm (½") in from the rim.

- Scatter the Mozzarella over the sauce and place sun-dried tomato strips evenly around.
- Dot goat's cheese throughout.

Place roast garlic between sun-dried tomato strips.

- Sprinkle over the Parmesan and chopped garlic
- Bake in the preheated oven for approx. 10 mins.
- Just after cooking brush with basil oil and garnish with fresh basil leaves.

PIZZA CLASSIC

As classic as could be. There's nothing to be said about this, other than when people began to understand that they could put cheese on pizzas, they always paired cheeses to emphasise the contrast of flavours between them. I've just taken two Italian cheeses with an Irish cheese, the ricotta salata being the salty contrast to the rich, full, creamy flavour of a soft Tipperary cream cheese.

INGREDIENTS

140g (5oz) basic pizza dough (SEE P. 17)
2 tablespoons basic tomato sauce (SEE P. 30)
55g (2oz) Mozzarella, grated
85g (3oz) cream cheese, crumbled
85g (3oz) ricotta salata, crumbled
15g (½ oz) Parmesan, freshly grated
1 clove garlic, very finely chopped

METHOD

PLACE PIZZA TILE on floor of the oven and preheat to maximum for one hour.

ASSEMBLING THE PIZZA

Stretch the dough into a 20cm (8") circle, spread the tomato sauce over the pizza 10mm (½") in from the rim.

- Scatter the Mozzarella evenly over the base of the pizza, dot with cream cheese and crumbled Ricotta.
- Sprinkle evenly with the Parmesan and garlic.
- Bake in the preheated oven for approx. 10 mins.

If you can't find Ricotta Salata, use Feta.

BLACK & BLUE

The Grubb family's Cashel Blue cheese, from Tipperary, and black olives are a great combination when cooked together. But it was the name which was the inspiration for this pizza, more than the ingredients. I remember standing in the kitchen of Patrick Clark's restaurant, Metro, in New York, and hearing the steaks being called "Black and Blue" – totally black on the outside and red raw in the centre.
Later I was making a pasta for myself, and I put in Cashel Blue and black olives, and I just loved the pairing so much that it seemed natural to make a pizza with those ingredients. The best olives to use are Niçoise.

INGREDIENTS

140g (5oz) basic pizza dough (SEE P. 17)
2 tablespoons basic tomato sauce (SEE P. 30)
(optional)
85g (3oz) Mozzarella, grated
115g (4oz) Cashel Blue, sliced
10 black olives
1 clove garlic, very finely chopped
25g (1oz) pistachio nuts (optional)

METHOD

PLACE PIZZA TILE on floor of the oven and preheat to maximum for one hour.

ASSEMBLING THE PIZZA Stretch the dough into a 20cm (8") circle.
- Spread the tomato sauce over the pizza 10mm (½") in from the rim.
- Scatter the Mozzarella evenly over the sauce followed by the Cashel Blue.
- Place the olives on top and sprinkle over the garlic and the pistachio nuts.
- Bake in the preheated oven for approx.10 mins.

A light, creamy Gorgonzola, instead of Cashel Blue, may be used and walnuts can be substituted for pistachio nuts.

OPPOSITE: LETTUCES GROWING AT EDEN PLANTS

HOT SPINACH PIZZA

In classical Indian cuisine, spinach and hot sauces always complement each other, and this is my interpretation of that in relation to pizza. Pizza is a melting pot for the traditions and flavourings of other countries, so it was natural for me to use it to interpret the flavours of the East.

INGREDIENTS

140g (5oz) basic pizza dough (SEE P. 17)
175g (6oz) cooked spinach
2 tablespoons hot chilli tomato sauce (SEE P. 31)
140g (5oz) goat's cheese, crumbled
1 clove garlic, very finely chopped (optional)

METHOD

PLACE PIZZA TILE on floor of the oven and preheat to maximum for one hour.

TO COOK SPINACH Wash thoroughly in three changes of water.
- Shake off excess water.
- Place the saucepan over a high heat.
- Cover, and when it begins to steam, toss the spinach.
- Turn the heat down low and allow the spinach to cook until tender.
- Squeeze out excess water.

ASSEMBLING THE PIZZA Stretch the dough into a 20cm (8") circle, spread the hot chilli tomato sauce over the pizza 10mm (1/2") in from the rim.
- Distribute the spinach on top.
- Dot with the goat's cheese and sprinkle on the garlic.
- Bake in the preheated oven for approx. 10 mins.

Alternatively, sauté 2 diced shallots in some oil, add 1/4 teaspoon garam masala. Add this to the cooked spinach. Sauté for another minute and use as above.

OPPOSITE: HOT SPINACH PIZZA

MUSHROOMS DRIED AND FRESH, WITH ROASTED TOMATOES #1

Everybody loves mushrooms, and this pizza is all about cooking them and getting the fabulous cooked mushroom flavour onto a pizza. Mushrooms have a distinctive flavour, especially if you are using dried mushrooms, so they need the contrast of the intensely flavoured tomatoes. Both the flavours are pronounced but they balance each other beautifully.

INGREDIENTS

140g (5oz) basic pizza dough (SEE P. 17)
40g (1½oz) dried Porcini mushrooms
2 cloves smoked garlic, minced
olive oil
140g (5oz) fresh mushrooms, sliced
salt and freshly ground black pepper
thyme oil or olive oil
8 oven roasted tomatoes, (SEE P. 36) sliced into strips
8 green olives
25g (1oz) Parmesan, freshly grated (optional)
1 tablespoon parsley, finely chopped
a generous mixture of thyme leaves
lemon wedges

METHOD

PLACE PIZZA TILE on floor of the oven and preheat to maximum for one hour.

RECONSTITUTING THE PORCINI Soak in luke warm water for 30 mins.
- Filter through a tea towel, reserving the liquid.
- Rinse thoroughly under cold water – drain and gently pat dry with tea towel.

COOKING THE MUSHROOMS Sauté 1 clove garlic in olive oil (reserving the other clove for the pizza) until soft, but do not brown.
- Add the fresh mushrooms and sauté until cooked.
- In another saucepan heat about 125ml (4fl oz, ½ cup) of the dried mushroom liquid and add the reconstituted mushrooms.
- Increase the heat and continue to cook until most of the liquid has evaporated.
- Add the porcini to the fresh mushrooms and remove from the heat. Season.

ASSEMBLING THE PIZZA Stretch the dough into a 20cm (8") circle.
- Brush the base with a light coat of thyme oil or olive oil.
- Top with the mushrooms.
- Arrange the oven roasted tomatoes and olives on top.
- Sprinkle with the Parmesan, the fresh herbs and the remaining chopped garlic.
- Bake in the preheated oven for approx. 10 mins.
- Garnish with lemon wedges.

MUSHROOMS DRIED AND FRESH, WITH ROASTED TOMATOES #2

Mushrooms absolutely love cheese, so it seemed natural to include cheese with this pizza. With mushroom pizza #1, I didn't use any cheese simply because the flavours were so good on their own. Here we go back to the classic pairing, and it's irresistible, friendly food, friendly flavours.

INGREDIENTS

140g (5oz) basic pizza dough (SEE P. 17)
40g (1½ oz) dried Porcini mushrooms
115g (4oz) fresh mushrooms, sliced
2 cloves smoked garlic, very finely chopped
olive oil
55g (2oz) butter
125ml (4fl oz, ½ cup) cream
25g (1oz) pistachio nuts, toasted and ground
salt and 1 teaspoon freshly ground black pepper
8 oven roasted tomatoes, sliced into strips
8 green olives
25g (1oz) Parma ham, torn into strips
1 tablespoon parsley, finely chopped with a generous mixture of thyme leaves
85g (3oz) Parmesan, freshly grated
lemon wedges (optional)
extra thyme leaves for garnish

METHOD

PLACE PIZZA TILE on floor of the oven and preheat to maximum for one hour.

RECONSTITUTING THE PORCINI See previous recipe.

COOKING THE MUSHROOMS Sauté 1 clove garlic in the olive oil and butter until soft.
- Add the fresh mushrooms and sauté until they give up their juices.
- In another saucepan heat about 125ml (4fl oz, ½ cup) of the dried mushroom liquid and add the reconstituted porcini.
- Increase the heat and cook until most of the liquid has evaporated.
- Add cream and cook until it reduces to become thick and binding.
- Season.
- Combine with the fresh mushrooms and add the toasted pistachios.
- Season, and allow to cool.

ASSEMBLING THE PIZZA Stretch the dough into a 20cm (8") circle.
- Spread the mushrooms over the pizza 10mm (½") in from the rim.
- Arrange the tomatoes, olives and the Parma ham on top.
- Sprinkle on the herbs, half the Parmesan and the reserved garlic.
- Bake for approx. 10 mins.
- About 3 mins before the pizza has finished cooking, add remaining Parmesan.
- Garnish with lemon and thyme.

FAVA BEAN, PECORINO AND ROCKET

On a trip to the south of Italy, I became totally addicted to fava beans, the broad bean as we call it. When I came home I made a salad with shaved Pecorino, rocket, fava beans and tossed greens, with a balsamic dressing, and then I made a pizza with these same ingredients. Understanding how you treat the bean is very important. When they are very young, you pop them out of the pods and pop them in your mouth. As they get a little older you have to blanch them, take off the outer skin, and get right in there to the bean itself. Sweet and delicious, and perfectly complemented by the Pecorino. It's a very light, summery pizza.

INGREDIENTS

140g (5oz) basic pizza dough (SEE P. 17)
olive oil
salt
1 clove garlic, very finely chopped
1 recipe fava bean cream (SEE P. 41)
6 oven roasted tomatoes
with black pepper (SEE P. 36)
rocket leaves, torn
55g (2oz) Pecorino, shaved
1 tablespoon balsamic vinegar

METHOD

PLACE PIZZA TILE on floor of the oven and preheat to maximum for one hour.

ASSEMBLING THE PIZZA Stretch the dough into a 20cm (8") circle.
■ Brush with olive oil, salt and garlic and partially bake in the preheated oven for about 3 minutes.
■ Take out of the oven and spread with the fava bean cream, leaving a 10mm (½") rim.
■ Arrange the tomatoes and reserved fava beans on top and return to the oven.
■ Cook for approx. another 7 mins.
■ Meanwhile toss the rocket in the balsamic vinegar.
■ Remove the pizza from the oven and scatter with the rocket and Pecorino.

Alternatively, bake the pizza blind and assemble the toppings when cold.
It's important to use a good quality Pecorino – if you can't find good Pecorino, use shaved mature Cratloe sheep cheese.

PIZZA MARGHERITA

There is a restaurant in Naples called Da Michele, one of the oldest pizza houses, where they only bake two types of pizza. Neapolitan and Pizza Margherita, and they are jam packed, making pizzas non-stop, all day long. Fabulous, beautiful flavours. I have never had a Margherita or a Neapolitan anywhere in the world which tastes anything like it. It is distinctly, completely, a Neapolitan activity. We can only try to emulate it, but we can never do more than that.

INGREDIENTS

140g (5oz) basic pizza dough (SEE P. 17)*
3 tablespoons basic tomato sauce (SEE P. 30)
55g (2oz) fresh, hand-rolled Mozzarella torn into pieces or diced
15g (½oz) Parmesan, freshly grated
1 clove garlic, very finely sliced
basil oil
8 fresh basil leaves
salt to taste

*omit the oil when making the dough

METHOD

PLACE PIZZA TILE on the floor of the oven and preheat to maximum for one hour.

ASSEMBLING THE PIZZA

- Stretch the dough into a 20cm (8") circle.
- Spread the tomato sauce over the pizza, 10mm (½") in from the rim.
- Scatter the Mozzarella slices on top of the sauce.
- Sprinkle on the Parmesan and garlic and drizzle with the basil oil.
- Bake in the preheated oven for approx. 10 mins.
- Serve garnished with the basil leaves.

CLASSIC NEAPOLITAN

Nothing to be said about it. It's been there since the fabulous people of Naples introduced the tomato to a pizza.

INGREDIENTS

140g (5oz) basic pizza dough (SEE P. 17))*
3 tablespoons basic tomato sauce (SEE P. 30)
¼ teaspoon dried oregano
2 cloves garlic, thinly sliced
Extra Virgin Olive Oil

*omit the oil when making the dough

METHOD

PLACE PIZZA TILE on the floor of the oven and preheat to maximum for one hour.

ASSEMBLING THE PIZZA

- Stretch the dough into a 20cm (8") circle.
- Spread the tomato sauce over the pizza 10mm (½") in from the rim.
- Sprinkle over the sliced garlic and dried oregano.
- Drizzle with olive oil.
- Bake in the preheated oven for approx. 10 mins.
- Remove from the oven and brush with the oil.

GORGONZOLA, SAUTÉED ONIONS & ROASTED POTATOES

Melted cheese on top of spuds (potatoes) is a flavour we are all familiar with. Initially I used Gorgonzola sparingly and wasn't totally convinced about it on its own on a pizza. I found its flavour a little bit too pointed, but here the starchy potatoes absorb the Gorgonzola, and this is one of my own personal favourite pizzas. Being Irish we just love to use spuds, which team up here with the sautéed onions, and it works fabulously.

INGREDIENTS

140g (5oz) basic pizza dough (SEE P. 17)
8 baby potatoes, scrubbed, left whole
olive oil
salt and pepper
fresh rosemary
2 onions, thinly sliced
2 tablespoons olive oil
115g (4oz) Gorgonzola, crumbled
1 clove garlic, very finely chopped

METHOD

PLACE PIZZA TILE on floor of the oven and preheat to maximum for one hour.

TO COOK THE POTATOES Place potatoes on a baking tray and toss in a little olive oil. Season with salt and pepper and add the rosemary.
- Bake in a very hot, 500°F, 240°C, Gas 9, oven until slightly brown.

TO COOK THE ONIONS Sauté the onions in the olive oil and season with salt and freshly ground black pepper.
- Cook until golden.
- Remove from the heat and allow to cool.

ASSEMBLING THE PIZZA Stretch the dough into a 20cm (8") circle.
- Spread the onions over the pizza 10mm (1/2") in from the rim and arrange the roast potatoes on top.
- Crumble the Gorgonzola over the pizza and sprinkle on the chopped garlic and rosemary leaves to taste.
- Bake in the preheated oven for approx. 10 mins.

CABBAGE PIZZA

What do the Irish like? Bacon and cabbage! What do the Irish eat? Bacon and cabbage! Or so we are told.
People do love it, and it was inevitable that I would ask: can I interpret this on a pizza? The answer was yes. The genius of this pizza is in the classical combination of a great Parma ham with well-flavoured cabbage.The funky idea, then, is the use of the pine nuts as both texture and for that nutty flavour which is an echo of the flavour of the cabbage, that hint of nutmeg. The little drizzle of truffle oil, added right at the end just before serving, is there because of the prosciutto: they are made for each other.

INGREDIENTS

140g (5oz) basic pizza dough (SEE P. 17)
175g (6oz) cabbage, shredded
40g (1½oz) butter
3 tablespoons cream
¼ teaspoon of nutmeg, grated
2 tablespoons basic tomato sauce (SEE P. 30)
40g (1½oz) Parmesan, freshly grated
70g (2½oz) Mozzarella, grated
115g (4oz) cream cheese, crumbled
25g (1oz) pinenuts
Parma ham
Truffle oil

METHOD

PLACE PIZZA TILE on floor of the oven and preheat to maximum for one hour.

TO PREPARE THE CABBAGE Cook and drain the cabbage and season with salt and pepper when still hot.
- Add the butter, cream and nutmeg and toss to combine.

ASSEMBLING THE PIZZA Stretch the dough into a 20cm (8") circle.
- Spread the tomato sauce over the pizza 10mm (½") in from the rim.
- Sprinkle with the Mozzarella, then the cabbage and dot with the cream cheese, sprinkle over Parmesan and finally the pine nuts.
- Bake in the preheated oven for approx. 10 mins.
- Remove from the oven and drape with thin slices of Parma and drizzle with truffle oil.

LA PROVENÇAL #1

Onion confit is a classical French flavour, you could almost say a classical French condiment. The combination of flavours in this pizza is one up from the Pissaladière. The goat's cheese is great with the confit – it's a beautiful contrast.

INGREDIENTS

140g (5oz) basic pizza dough (SEE P. 17)
175g (6oz, 3/4 cup) onion confit (SEE P. 40)
175g (6oz) goat's cheese
2 tomatoes, thinly sliced
10 black olives
1 clove garlic, very finely chopped
1 teaspoon thyme leaves

METHOD

PLACE PIZZA TILE on the floor of the oven and preheat to maximum for one hour.

ASSEMBLING THE PIZZA Stretch the dough into a 20cm (8") circle.
- Spread the onion confit over the pizza 10mm (1/2") in from the rim.
- Dot the goat's cheese on the confit and arrange the tomatoes and olives on top.
- Scatter over the garlic and thyme.
- Bake in the preheated oven for approx. 10 mins.

LA PROVENÇAL #2

While the first pizza is more orthodox, this second Provençal pizza uses both tomato sauce and Mozzarella, for those who like to always use them on a pizza.

INGREDIENTS

140g (5oz) basic pizza dough (SEE P. 17)
175g (6oz, 3/4 cup) onion confit (SEE P. 40)
2 tomatoes, thinly sliced
10 olives
1 clove garlic, very finely chopped
2 tablespoons basic tomato sauce (SEE P. 30)
85g (3oz) fresh Mozzarella (optional)
140g (5oz) goat's cheese
1 teaspoon thyme leaves

METHOD

PLACE PIZZA TILE on the floor of the oven and preheat to maximum for one hour.

ASSEMBLING THE PIZZA Stretch the dough into a 20cm (8") circle.
- Spread the tomato sauce over the pizza 10mm (1/2") in from the rim and top with the Mozzarella.
- Place the tomato slices at the outer edge of the pizza, making sure not to overlap.
- Pile the confit in the centre of the pizza.
- Crumble the goat's cheese around.
- Arrange the olives on top and sprinkle with the thyme and chopped garlic.
- Bake in the preheated oven for approx. 10 mins.

OPPOSITE: LA PROVENÇAL PIZZA. OVERLEAF: CABBAGE PIZZA (SEE P. 67), GORGONZOLA & ROASTED POTATO PIZZA (SEE P. 66)

MILLEENS PIZZA

This is one step up from a Pizza baked blind. It doesn't have a sauce, it doesn't have Mozzarella, it doesn't have any of the traditional things you associate with a pizza.

When Milleens is cooked and melts, it has a buttery, slightly nutty, sharp taste and the perfect pairing for that is sun-dried tomatoes, and a glut of soft herbs on top, always soft herbs: yellow marjoram, sweet marjoram, basil and oregano. These suit the herbaceousness of one of the great West Cork cheeses.

INGREDIENTS

140g (5oz) basic pizza dough (SEE P. 17)
basil oil or sun-dried tomato oil
85g (3oz) sundried tomatoes, excess oil squeezed out, shredded into strips
85g (3oz) cream cheese
85g (3oz) Milleens cheese, very finely sliced
fresh herbs (marjoram, oregano, basil, yellow marjoram, lemon thyme etc)
rosemary oil or sun-dried tomato oil

METHOD

PLACE PIZZA TILE on floor of the oven and preheat to maximum for one hour.

ASSEMBLING THE PIZZA Stretch the dough into a 20cm (8") circle.

- Brush the surface with basil oil, or sun-dried tomato oil.
- Scatter the sundried tomatoes on top of the base.
- Dot with cream cheese to prevent from burning.
- Cover with Milleens.
- Bake in the preheated oven for approx. 10 mins.
- After cooking brush the outer edge of the pizza with either rosemary oil or olive oil from the sun-dried tomatoes and scatter over a generous amount of the fresh herbs.

OPPOSITE: MILLEENS PIZZA

HOT CHILLI PIZZA

This is eastern hot food meeting California, this is a complete Fusion Food pairing: the sun-dried tomatoes with hot chillies, a silky soft cheese, and loads of coriander. It's great with oven roasted tomatoes.

INGREDIENTS

140g (5oz) basic pizza dough (SEE P. 17)
2 tablespoons hot chilli sauce
85g (3oz) Mozzarella, grated
55g (2oz) sun-dried tomatoes torn into strips
85g (3oz) cream cheese
1 clove garlic, very finely chopped
2 teaspoons olive oil
Bunch of fresh coriander
hot chilli oil (optional)

METHOD

PLACE PIZZA TILE on the floor of the oven and preheat to maximum for one hour.

ASSEMBLING THE PIZZA

- Stretch the dough into a 20cm (8") circle.
- Spread the hot chilli sauce over the pizza 10mm (1/2") in from the rim.
- Scatter over the Mozzarella.
- Arrange the sun-dried tomatoes on top and cover with the cream cheese.
- Finally sprinkle with the garlic and drizzle with the olive oil.
- Bake in the preheated oven for approx. 10 min.
- Serve garnished with plenty of fresh coriander and some hot chilli oil.

FOUR CHEESE PIZZA

A simple, classic pizza, using three of the great Italian cheeses.

INGREDIENTS

140g (5oz) basic pizza dough (SEE P. 17)
2 tablespoons tomato sauce (SEE P. 30) (optional)
55g (2oz) Mozzarella, grated
85g (3oz) cream cheese
55g (2oz) Gorgonzola
1 clove garlic, very finely chopped
15g (1/2 oz) Parmesan, freshly grated

METHOD

PLACE PIZZA TILE on the floor of the oven and preheat to maximum for one hour.

ASSEMBLING THE PIZZA

- Stretch the dough into a 20cm (8") circle.
- Spread the tomato sauce over the pizza 10mm (1/2") in from the rim.
- Scatter the Mozzarella evenly over the base of the pizza.
- Dot with the cream cheese and Gorgonzola.
- Scatter over the Parmesan, and distribute the garlic evenly over the cheese.
- Bake in the preheated oven for approx. 10 mins.

IRISH CHEESEBOARD PIZZA

In "The Irish Times" there was a map of Ireland with the farmhouse cheeses from all around the country and I thought, hey, I've got five of those on a pizza and so I decided to add two more, and there I had my Irish cheeseboard.

INGREDIENTS

140g (5oz) basic pizza dough (SEE P. 17)
2 tablespoons basic tomato sauce (SEE P. 30)
175g (6oz) Irish Mozzarella, grated
70g (2½oz) Cashel Blue
40g (1½oz) St Tola goat's log
70g (2½oz) Cooleeney
85g (3oz) Compsey cream cheese
70g (2½oz) Compsey cottage cheese
70g (2½oz) Smoked Gubbeen
2 cloves garlic, very finely chopped

METHOD

PLACE PIZZA TILE on floor of the oven and preheat to maximum for one hour.

ASSEMBLING THE PIZZA Stretch the dough into a 20cm (8") circle.
▪ Spread the tomato sauce over the pizza 10mm (½") inch in from the rim, leaving the middle underfilled as the melting cheese will slide to the centre during baking.
▪ Sprinkle over the Mozzarella to line the pizza.
▪ Assemble the remaining six cheeses, giving each its own portion of the pie, so maintaining the distinctive flavours.
▪ Sprinkle with the chopped garlic.
▪ Bake in the preheated oven for approx. 10 mins.

THE PIZZAS

FISH & SHELLFISH PIZZAS

SMOKED SALMON PIZZA

One of the first pizzas I ever put on the menu was smoked salmon pizza. We have fabulous smoked salmon in Ireland and so it was inevitable I would use it. The contrast in flavours is between mild and beautiful cheese and counter balancing that are fresh chives, and scallions.

INGREDIENTS

140g (5oz) basic pizza dough (SEE P. 17)
2 tablespoons of basic tomato sauce (SEE P. 30) (optional)
70g (2½oz) smoked salmon, sliced into thin strips
55g (2oz) cottage cheese
1 tablespoon chives, chopped
2 scallions, thinly sliced
25g (1oz) Parmesan, freshly grated
70g (2½oz) cream cheese, crumbled
85g (3oz) Mozzarella, grated
1 clove garlic, very finely chopped

METHOD

PLACE PIZZA TILE on the floor of the oven and preheat to maximum for one hour.

ASSEMBLING THE PIZZA Stretch the dough into a 20cm (8") circle.
- If you are using tomato sauce spread it over the pizza 10mm (½") in from the rim.
- Scatter over the Mozzarella.
- Arrange the salmon strips on the pizza and dot with the cottage cheese and cream cheese.
- Evenly distribute the minced garlic, the chives and scallions and Parmesan on top.
- Bake in the preheated oven for approx. 10 mins.

ROQUEFORT & SMOKED SALMON

The pairing of these two very strongly flavoured ingredients may seem very odd. For me it was a response to being in both France and Italy, particularly Rome and the Marches, where they love strong flavours, gutsy, hearty, strong flavours that we would scarcely endure. Their cooking is natural and earthy, so the pairing of the strong Roquefort with the smoked salmon was just a response to that, for those who want really gutsy, strong flavours. Not for the delicate palate.

INGREDIENTS

140g (5oz) basic pizza dough (SEE P. 17)
2 tablespoons basic tomato sauce (SEE P. 30)
85g (3oz) Mozzarella, grated
85g (3oz) smoked salmon torn into strips
115g (4oz) Roquefort cheese
100g (3½oz) cream cheese
1 clove garlic, very finely chopped
25g (1oz) Parmesan, freshly grated

METHOD

PLACE PIZZA TILE on the floor of the oven and preheat to maximum for one hour.

ASSEMBLING THE PIZZA Stretch the dough into a 20cm (8") circle.
- Spread the tomato sauce over the pizza 10mm (½") in from the rim.
- Scatter the Mozzarella over the pizza, and arrange smoked salmon on top.
- Dot both Roquefort and cream cheese throughout.
- Sprinkle on the fresh garlic.
- Bake in the preheated oven for approx. 10 mins.
- Sprinkle Parmesan over the baked pizza and serve immediately.

FRESH PRAWN PIZZA

This is a real people-pleaser. You must use fresh prawns, as fresh as you can possibly get, because otherwise their flavour is lost. Garlic, parsley and prawns are a great trio. Alternatively, you could also heat a little oil and add in some strands of saffron, then toss the prawns, garlic and parsley in the oil before placing on the pizza. The sweetness of the prawns and the saffron is bliss.

INGREDIENTS

140g (5oz) basic pizza dough (SEE P. 17)
225g (8oz) fresh prawns removed from the shell
olive oil
1½ tablespoons flat leaf parsley, chopped
1 teaspoon garlic, very finely chopped
2 tablespoons tomato and fennel sauce (SEE P. 30)
85g (3oz) Mozzarella, grated
85g (3oz) cream cheese
25g (1oz) Parmesan, freshly grated
fresh chervil

METHOD

PLACE PIZZA TILE on the floor of the oven and preheat to maximum for one hour.

PREPARING THE PRAWNS Before you begin to assemble the pizza, toss the prawns in a little olive oil, the parsley and garlic.

ASSEMBLING THE PIZZA Stretch the dough into a 20cm (8") circle.

- Spread the tomato and fennel sauce over the pizza 10mm (½") in from the rim and top with the Mozzarella making sure to cover all of the sauce.
- Dot the cream cheese on the pizza and bake in the preheated oven for approx. 7 mins.
- Take the pizza out, dress with the prawns and sprinkle over the Parmesan.
- Bake for a further 2-3 minutes.
- Serve garnished with fresh chervil.

SMOKED HADDOCK WITH A THREE ONION SAUCE & NEW POTATOES

This pizza is an echo of the tradition of "Fish on Friday", with boiled potatoes and the infamous white onion sauce. This, however, is far from penitential food.

INGREDIENTS

140g (5oz) basic pizza dough (SEE P. 17)
115g (4oz) smoked haddock, skinned
1 tsp tarragon mustard mixed with 1 tsp water, or 2 tsps tarragon marinade (SEE GLOSSARY)
3 new potatoes
olive oil, thyme, salt and black pepper
115g (4oz) shallots, diced
25g (1oz) chives, finely sliced
85g (3oz) scallions, finely sliced
1 small white turnip, 1 teaspoon lemon juice

METHOD

PLACE PIZZA TILE on the floor of the oven and preheat to maximum for one hour.

- Slice fish into 10mm (½") thick medallions.
- Toss in the marinade.
- Drizzle potatoes with oil, scatter on thyme, season and bake until just cooked. Slice in two.
- To make the sauce: sauté the onions in a little oil making sure not to brown them.
- Remove from the heat and season.
- Grate the turnip and toss in lemon juice.

ASSEMBLING THE PIZZA

- Spread the onion sauce over the pizza 10mm (½") in from the rim.
- Top with the potatoes, cut sides up, and in between place the haddock and cover with the grated turnip.
- Bake in the preheated oven for approx. 10 mins.

SEAFOOD PIZZA #1

One morning, worn out from the previous night's work, I was walking along the strand at Cooleenamore, enjoying the magnificence of the mountain and the sea, and there, at my feet, was free food: cockles and mussels. I adore them.
Whenever I have the chance, I pick cockles and mussels, and I add clams when I can get them. I created the fennel sauce because shellfish loves the flavour of aniseed.

INGREDIENTS

140g (5oz) basic pizza dough (SEE P. 17)
85g (3oz) cockle meat
85g (3oz) mussels
55g (2oz) clams
4 oysters
2 tablespoons tomato & fennel sauce (SEE P. 30)
1 tablespoon parsley, chopped
1 clove garlic, very finely chopped

METHOD

PLACE PIZZA TILE on the floor of the oven and preheat to maximum for one hour.

PREPARING THE SHELLFISH Steam open the cockles, mussels and clams.
- Remove from their shells and toss in the parsley and garlic.
- Carefully open the oysters, removing any shell. Place in a bowl and reserve.

ASSEMBLING THE PIZZA Stretch the dough into a 20cm (8") circle.
- Spread the tomato and fennel sauce over 10mm (½") in from the rim and place in the preheated oven for 5mins.
- Take out and top with the mussels, clams and cockles.
- Continue to cook for a further 3-4 minutes.
- Place oysters on top and serve immediately.

NOTE The measurements given are for shellfish meat, not including shells.

SEAFOOD PIZZA #2

The same very natural, very simple, clean, fresh flavours. Shellfish pairs equally well with smoked Mozzarella. Hence this second seafood pizza.

INGREDIENTS

140g (5oz) basic pizza dough (SEE P. 17)
85g (3oz) cockle meat
85g (3oz) smoked mussels
55g (2oz) clams
4 oysters
1 tablespoon fennel and tomato sauce (SEE P. 30)
1 tablespoon parsley, chopped
1 clove garlic, very finely chopped
55g (2oz) smoked Mozzarella, thinly sliced
55g (2oz) cream cheese, crumbled
25g (1oz) Parmesan, freshly grated

METHOD

PLACE PIZZA TILE on the floor of the oven and preheat to maximum for one hour.
- Steam open the cockles, mussels and clams. Remove from the shells.

ASSEMBLING THE PIZZA Stretch the dough into a 20cm (8") circle.
- Spread the tomato and fennel sauce over the pizza 10mm (½") in from the rim.
- Top with the Mozzarella and the clams, mussels and cockles.
- Dot with the cream cheese.
- Sprinkle with the garlic and parsley.
- Bake in the preheated oven for approx. 10 mins.
- Open the oysters and add to the pizza in the last 3 mins.
- After cooking sprinkle over the grated Parmesan and serve immediately.

OPPOSITE: SEAFOOD PIZZA. OVERLEAF: BERNADETTE ON COOLEENAMORE STRAND

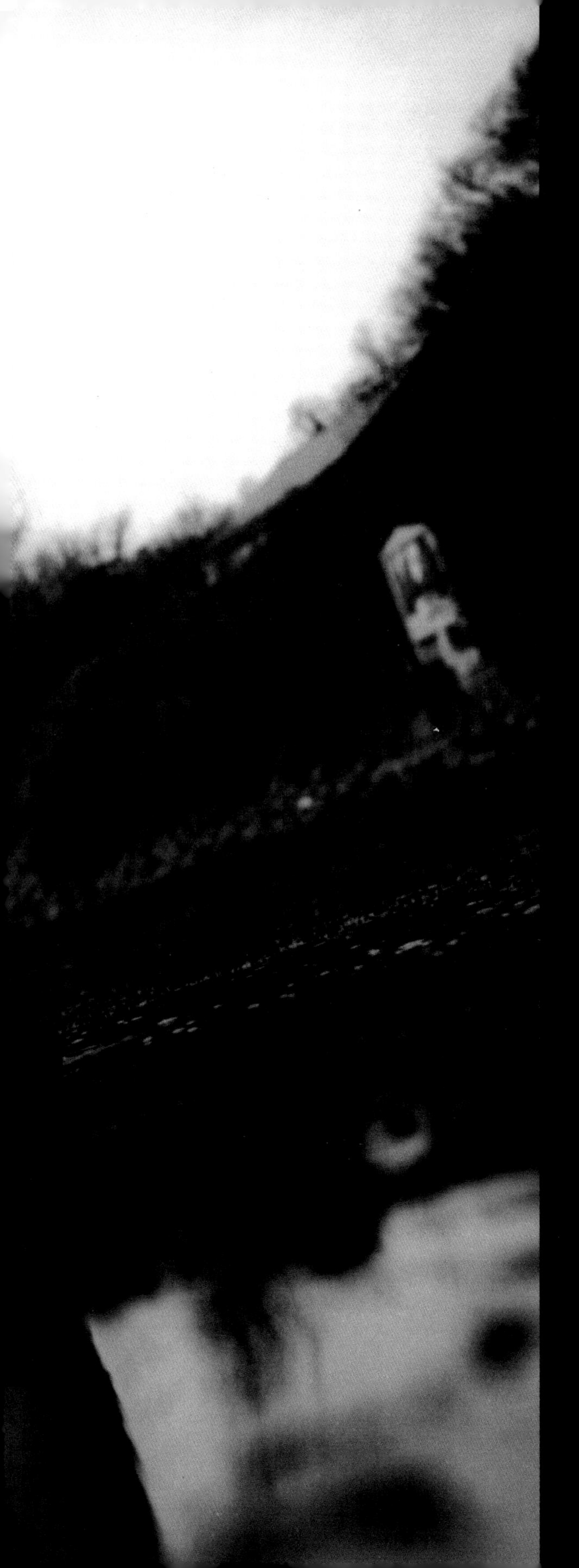

“

One morning, worn out from the previous night’s work, I was walking along the strand at Cooleenamore, enjoying the magnificence of the mountain and the sea, and there, at my feet, was free food: cockles and mussels.

I ADORE THEM

”

SAUSAGE PIZZAS

WE HAVE WONDERFUL PORK IN IRELAND, but we have never had a great sausage making tradition. I love sausages and think sausage on pizzas is fabulous. I started to make my own, and met a wonderful butcher – Grays of Sligo – who would supply me in the quantities I wanted, and so I set to work to make sausages that I thought would work great on a pizza.

MAKE SURE TO USE ONLY BACK FAT FOR THESE SAUSAGES – it's particularly soft and succulent – and use lean meat from the neck or shoulder. Ask the butcher to mince it very finely or use the fine blade in a hand cranked meat mincer.
These sausage meat recipes may be used without previous cooking. When ready to bake simply dot pizza with the raw sausage meat mixture.

HOWEVER, I LIKE TO COOK THE SAUSAGE MEAT IN ADVANCE because of the different texture, because the flavours are more evenly combined and developed and because it leaves a little fat behind in the pan so there is less oil on the pizza. It is also much easier to spread on the pizza.

OPPOSITE: GINGER SAUSAGE PIZZA

GINGER SAUSAGE

INGREDIENTS

115g (4oz) hardback fat, very finely minced together with 225g (8oz) lean pork (neck or shoulder)
40g (1½oz) fresh root ginger, minced
4 scallions thinly sliced
1½ tablespoons ground ginger
1½ teaspoons salt
1 tablespoon olive oil

METHOD

Using your fingers or a wooden spoon, combine all of the ingredients, except the oil ■ Heat the oil and add the sausage meat ■ Break up the mixture with a wooden spoon, making sure that lumps do not form when cooking ■ Sauté for about 10 mins over a moderate heat ■ Transfer to a bowl and allow to cool.

HOMEMADE HOT SAUSAGE

INGREDIENTS

115g (4oz) hardback fat, very finely minced together with 225g (8oz) lean pork (neck or shoulder)
1 medium onion, finely chopped
1 teaspoon ground coriander
1 tablespoon ground cumin
1 heaped teaspoon cayenne pepper
1 red chilli, sliced
1 teaspoon salt
1 tablespoon olive oil

METHOD

Sauté the onion in olive oil over medium heat ■ Add the spices and one minute later the meat ■ Using two wooden spoons, incorporate the onion and the spices into the pork ■ Continue to cook for 10 mins ■ Cool completely.

If you wish to use this sausage uncooked on the pizza then combine the raw ingredients together as you would the other recipes.

HERB SAUSAGE

INGREDIENTS

115g (4oz) hardback fat, very finely minced together with 225g (8oz) lean pork (neck or shoulder)
2 teaspoons fresh parsley, chopped
2 teaspoons fresh chives, finely sliced
1 medium onion, finely chopped
a good bunch of thyme
1 tablespoon olive oil
salt and pepper

METHOD

Using your fingers or a wooden spoon, combine all of the ingredients, except the oil ■ Heat the oil and add the sausage meat ■ Break up the mixture with a wooden spoon, making sure that lumps do not form when cooking ■ Sauté for about 10 mins over a moderate heat ■ Transfer to a bowl and allow to cool.

FENNEL SAUSAGE

INGREDIENTS

115g (4oz) hardback fat, very finely minced together with 225g (8oz) lean pork (neck or shoulder)
2 tablespoons ground fennel
1 teaspoon salt
85g (3oz) fresh fennel, finely sliced
1 tablespoon olive oil

METHOD

Using your fingers or a wooden spoon, combine all of the ingredients, except the oil ■ Heat the oil and add the sausage meat ■ Break up the mixture with a wooden spoon, making sure that lumps do not form when cooking ■ Sauté for about 10 minutes over a moderate heat ■ Transfer to a bowl and allow to cool.

FENNEL SAUSAGE PIZZA

This was the first sausage pizza I made for the restaurant and always the most popular. I love the sweet fennel flavour. The first time I ever came across it was when Evelyn Slomon made a fennel sausage. I didn't get the recipe and when I came home and started playing with it I came up with a more defined flavour. Also I cooked the sausage before I put it on the pizza, because I found that the flavours were far more developed and intense when cooked.

INGREDIENTS

140g (5oz) basic pizza dough (SEE P. 17)
2 tablespoons basic tomato sauce (SEE P. 30)
55g (2oz) Mozzarella, grated
225g (8oz) fennel sausage (SEE P. 87)
85g (3oz) cream cheese
25g (1oz) Parmesan, freshly grated
1 clove garlic, very finely chopped
fresh fennel, shaved, for garnish

METHOD

PLACE PIZZA TILE on the floor of the oven and preheat to maximum for one hour.

ASSEMBLING THE PIZZA

- Stretch the dough into a 20cm (8") circle.
- Spread the tomato sauce over the pizza 10mm (1/2") in from the rim.
- Sprinkle over the Mozzarella, followed by the sausage, the cream cheese and then the Parmesan.
- Finally sprinkle over the garlic.
- Bake in the preheated oven for approx. 10 mins.
- Garnish with shaved, fresh fennel.

GINGER SAUSAGE PIZZA

This was a response, on a November evening, to a salad of some Japanese leaves which had come from Eden Plants. It was delicious, and I thought, what do the Japanese love? Ginger. So I made the sausage using ginger and a natural complement to that was honey, just a little drizzle, not sweet and sour, I'm very sparing in the use of honey on this.

INGREDIENTS

140g (5oz) basic pizza dough (SEE P. 17)
2 tablespoons basic tomato sauce (SEE P. 30)
55g (2oz) Mozzarella, grated
225g (8oz) ginger sausage (SEE P.86)
85g (3oz) cream cheese
1 clove garlic, very finely chopped
1 teaspoon ginger, very finely chopped
1/2 teaspoon honey
fresh chives

METHOD

PLACE PIZZA TILE on the floor of the oven and preheat to maximum for one hour.

ASSEMBLING THE PIZZA

- Stretch the dough into a 20cm (8") circle.
- Spread the tomato sauce over the pizza 10mm (1/2") in from the rim.
- Sprinkle over the Mozzarella, followed by the sausage, the cream cheese and then the garlic and ginger.
- Bake in the preheated oven for approx. 10 mins.
- Garnish with the honey and fresh chives.

HERB SAUSAGE & ONION PURÉE WITH ROSEMARY POTATOES

The inspiration for this came from Germany and the great beer halls, where they always serve a good herb sausage, always paired with onions and potatoes. So then I added some rosemary, and the drizzle of sour cream is something which they automatically do. Germans love strong herb flavours and I created this pizza because we love those sorts of herby flavours as well.

INGREDIENTS

140g (5oz) basic pizza dough (SEE P. 17)
2 small potatoes
olive oil
1½ clove garlic, minced
fresh rosemary
2 generous tablespoons onion purée (SEE P. 40)
175g (6oz) herb sausage (SEE P. 87)
85g (3oz) cream cheese
15g (½oz) Parmesan, freshly grated
fresh thyme leaves
Sour cream

METHOD

PLACE PIZZA TILE on floor of the oven and preheat to maximum for one hour.

TO PREPARE THE POTATOES Parboil then peel and slice.
- Heat a little oil in a small skillet, add the potatoes, ½ clove garlic and rosemary leaves.
- Brown the potatoes and set aside.

ASSEMBLING THE PIZZA Stretch the dough into a 20cm (8") circle.
- Spread the onion purée over the pizza 10mm (½") in from the rim.
- Cover with the herb sausage.
- Arrange the potato slices on top and dot with the cream cheese.
- Sprinkle on the Parmesan, fresh thyme and the remaining garlic.
- Bake in the preheated oven for approx. 10 mins.
- Serve with sour cream on the side.

This pizza can be made with or without cheese. To make without cheese simply increase the onion sauce on the base and substitute extra sausage to compensate for the cheese.

HOT SAUSAGE PIZZA WITH PEACH & CARRAGEEN RELISH

This sausage was an instant, total, success, even though we had to warn people that it would blow their heads off because hot sausage means hot sausage. We have fabulous pork in Ireland and the other thing we have, in excess and abundance, is seaweed and so I paired this with a condiment, a salsa, of carrageen and peach. We are beginning to use seaweeds more and more. Seaweeds are nutritionally very good for us, and are being sourced in fresh water, clean sea waters, and we haven't even begun to understand the impact they are going to have on our cuisine over the next five years.

INGREDIENTS

140g (5oz) basic pizza dough (SEE P. 17)
2 tablespoons tomato sauce (SEE P. 30) or tomato and ginger sauce (SEE P. 31)
225g (8oz) home made hot sausage (SEE P. 86)
2 tomatoes, thinly sliced
1 clove garlic, very finely chopped
fresh coriander
70g (2½oz) Mozzarella (optional)
Peach and Carrageen Relish (SEE P. 123)

METHOD

PLACE PIZZA TILE on floor of the oven and preheat to maximum for one hour.

ASSEMBLING THE PIZZA Stretch the dough into a 20cm (8") circle.
- Spread the tomato sauce over the pizza 10mm (½") in from the rim.
- Sprinkle the Mozzarella (optional) evenly over and add the sausage.
- Arrange the tomato slices on top of the pizza, making sure not to overlap.
- Finally sprinkle with the chopped garlic.
- Bake in the preheated oven for approx. 10 mins.
- Serve with plenty of fresh coriander and with the Peach and Carrageen Relish.

PIZZA PEPPERONI

A classical, favourite ingredient on a pizza. Look out for the hung, dried, hard pepperonis, and avoid the vac-packed variety. There are several varieties of pepperoni available, and you can happily mix the varieties on the pizza.

INGREDIENTS

140g (5oz) basic pizza dough (SEE P. 17)
2 tablespoons tomato sauce (SEE P. 30)
85g (3oz) Mozzarella, grated
1 or more Pepperoni sausage, thinly sliced
85g (3oz) cream cheese
40g (1½oz) Parmesan
1 teaspoon chopped garlic

METHOD

PLACE PIZZA TILE on the floor of the oven and preheat to maximum for one hour.

ASSEMBLING THE PIZZA

- Stretch the dough into a 20cm (8") circle.
- Spread the tomato sauce over the pizza 10mm (½") in from the rim.
- Top with the Mozzarella making sure to cover the sauce.
- Scatter the pepperoni on the pizza.
- Dot with the cream cheese and sprinkle on the Parmesan and garlic.
- Bake in the preheated oven for approx. 10 mins.

A variety of salami can also be used in place of the Pepperoni.

NATURALLY SMOKED

My inspiration was utterly and entirely the wonderful smoked Gubbeen cheese, from Schull, in West Cork. When I got it I thought, Oh, I'll pair this with a smoked sausage. They work brilliantly together.

INGREDIENTS

140g (5oz) basic pizza dough (SEE P. 17)
2 tablespoons tomato sauce (SEE P. 30)
55g (2oz) Mozzarella, grated
1 dried smoked sausage very thinly sliced
85g (3oz) smoked Gubbeen
1 clove garlic, minced

METHOD

PLACE PIZZA TILE on the floor of the oven and preheat to maximum for one hour.

ASSEMBLING THE PIZZA

- Stretch the dough into a 20cm (8") circle.
- Spread the tomato sauce over the pizza 10mm (½") in from the rim.
- Top with the Mozzarella making sure to cover the sauce.
- Distribute the sausage on the pizza.
- Cover with the Gubbeen cheese and sprinkle on the garlic.
- Bake in the preheated oven for approx. 10 mins.

LEEK & BLACK PUDDING PIZZA

This pizza was my response to the clutch of new recipes which were part of the nouvelle cuisine in Ireland, when age-old ingredients such as black pudding were "outed", it was one of those outed ingredients. I remember as a child my mother making black pudding and my father frying either onions or leeks which we always ate with the pudding. I love the look of the pizza. I use Clonakilty black pudding and there's nothing to beat it, with beautiful, small young leeks, drizzled with a good strong rosemary oil. I use Mascarpone because it doesn't interfere with the flavour, shape or style of the other ingredients.

INGREDIENTS

140g (5oz) basic pizza dough (SEE P. 17)
115g (4oz) leeks, sliced
olive oil
salt and pepper
2 tablespoons mascarpone
140g (5oz) black pudding, sliced
25g (1oz) pine nuts
rosemary oil (SEE P. 122)

METHOD

PLACE PIZZA TILE on floor of the oven. Protect the base of your oven with cooking foil (if this pizza leaks it burns, prepare youself for smoke!) Preheat the oven to its maximum temperature.

TO COOK THE LEEKS Sauté the sliced leeks in a little olive oil until tender.
- Alternatively toss in a little olive oil, place on a baking tray and cook in a hot oven.
- When cooked, season with salt and pepper, and allow to cool.

ASSEMBLING THE PIZZA Stretch the dough into a 20cm (8") circle.
- Gently spread on the mascarpone with your fingers, making sure to leave a 1cm (½") rim all around.
- Pile the leeks in the centre.
- Circle the pizza with the black pudding slices and scatter the pine nuts in between the black pudding and the leek.
- Bake in the preheated oven for approx. 10 mins.
- Drizzle with rosemary oil and serve.

OPPOSITE: LEAK & BLACK PUDDING PIZZA. OVERLEAF: HOT SAUSAGE PIZZA (SEE P. 90)

CALZONE

Calzone is essentially **A FOLDED PIZZA** one side of it is stuffed and you use the other half of the pizza to fold over the stuffing. You then crimp it together and you have your Calzone.

IT'S COMPLETELY DIFFERENT TO PIZZA, it's very filling, it's like supper food rather than dinner food.

Calzone is never served on its own so I serve it with a green salad and a sauce on the side, a tomato sauce or a hot chilli sauce.

The way in which Calzone cooks is completely differently from a pizza. Everything inside is pre-cooked and the suspended moisture of the ingredients is protected from direct heat. You must fully stuff the calzone – there should be no pockets of air. If it is well stuffed the dough will still have texture.

The filling inside should be warm to hot when the dough is cooked. It's a gutsy, hearty meal, and you can't share it.

IT'S NOT FOR SHARING.

PREVIOUS PAGE: STROMBOLI BREAD (SEE P. 101). OPPOSITE: CALZONE

CALZONE PESTO

INGREDIENTS

140g (5oz) basic pizza dough (SEE P. 17)
2 tablespoons home made pesto (SEE P. 40)
140g (5oz) goat's cheese
55g (2oz) Parmesan, freshly grated
25g (1oz) Mozzarella, grated
8 basil leaves, plus extra serving
sun-dried tomato oil or olive oil

METHOD

PLACE PIZZA TILE on the floor of the oven and preheat to maximum for one hour.

ASSEMBLING THE CALZONE
- Stretch the dough into a 20cm (8") circle.
- Place the filling over one half of the circle, making sure to leave a clean 10mm (½") rim and then layer one ingredient on top of another.
- Begin the filling with a layer of Mozzarella.
- Top with the goat's cheese, the pesto, the Parmesan and finally the torn basil leaves.
- Fold the empty half of the dough over the ingredients and press the outer edges together with your fingers.
- Bake for approx. 20 mins in the hottest oven.
- Check after 10 mins, and cover with tin foil if it browns too quickly.
- When cooked remove from oven and brush with sun-dried tomato oil or olive oil.

Serve with a green salad, warmed basic tomato sauce and a side dish of tomato concasse. (Skin and seed some tomatoes, slice into small dice. Sprinkle with salt, a little good quality olive oil and fresh basil leaves.)

CALZONE WITH LEEK, GOAT'S CHEESE & PARMA HAM

INGREDIENTS

140g (5oz) basic pizza dough (SEE P. 17)
40g (1½oz) Mozzarella, grated
140g (5oz) cooked leeks
55g (2oz) Parma ham, torn into strips
25g (1oz) Parmesan, freshly grated
1 teaspoon fresh thyme leaves
140g (5oz) goat's cheese
olive oil

METHOD

PLACE PIZZA TILE on the floor of the oven and preheat to maximum for one hour.

TO COOK THE LEEKS Sauté the sliced leeks in a little olive oil until tender.
- Season with salt and pepper.
- Allow to cool.

ASSEMBLING THE CALZONE Stretch the dough into a 20cm (8") circle.
- Place the filling over one half of the circle, making sure to leave a clean 10mm (½") rim and then layer one ingredient on top of another.
- Begin the filling with a layer of Mozzarella, top with the leeks, strips of Parma ham, the Parmesan, thyme and finally the goat's cheese.
- Fold the empty half of the dough over the ingredients and press the outer edges together with your fingers.
- Bake for approx. 20 mins in the hottest oven.
- Check after 10 mins, and cover with tin foil if it browns too quickly.
- When cooked immediately brush with olive oil.

Serve with warmed basic tomato sauce and greens.

CALZONE SPINACH & THREE CHEESES

INGREDIENTS

140g (5oz) basic pizza dough (SEE P. 17)
25g (1oz) pine nuts
175g (6oz) cooked spinach
55g (2oz) Mozzarella, grated
55g (2oz) Parmesan, freshly grated
55g (2oz) cream cheese, crumbled

METHOD

PLACE PIZZA TILE on the floor of the oven and preheat to maximum for one hour.

PREPARING THE FILLING Roast the nuts in a hot oven for about 5 mins.
▪ Place in the bowl of a food processor and process until smooth.
▪ Wash the spinach thoroughly in three changes of water.
▪ Shake off excess water.
▪ Place in a saucepan over a high heat.
▪ Cover, and toss when it begins to steam.
▪ Turn the heat down low and allow to cook until tender.
▪ Remove from pan and squeeze out excess water.

ASSEMBLING THE CALZONE Stretch the dough into a 20cm (8") circle.
▪ Place the filling over one half of the circle, making sure to leave a clean 10mm (½") rim and then layer one ingredient on top of another.
▪ Begin with a layer of Mozzarella, top with the spinach, Parmesan, cream cheese and then the ground pine nuts.
▪ Fold the empty half of the dough over the ingredients and press the outer edges together with your fingers.
▪ Bake for approx. 20 mins in hottest oven.
▪ Check after 10 mins, and cover with tin foil if it browns too quickly.
▪ When cooked remove from oven and brush with olive oil.
Serve with a green salad or a relish of natural yogurt and toasted almonds.
Two tablespoons of hot chilli sauce may be added to the calzone (on top of the spinach) or served on the side.

CALZONE ONION & POTATO

INGREDIENTS

140g (5oz) basic pizza dough (SEE P. 17)
2 small onions, thinly sliced
2 small potatoes, thinly sliced
1 tablespoon thyme
butter
140g (5oz) goat's cheese
salt and freshly ground black pepper
1 egg
50ml (2 floz, ¼ cup) sour cream

METHOD

PLACE PIZZA TILE on the floor of the oven and preheat to maximum for one hour.

PREPARING THE FILLING Cook the onions in a little olive oil.
▪ Add the potatoes and sauté together with the thyme and a little butter.
▪ Season with salt and black pepper and allow to cool.
▪ Lightly beat the egg in a bowl and add the potato mixture, the goat's cheese and the cream.

ASSEMBLING THE CALZONE Stretch the dough into a 20cm (8") circle.
▪ Place the potato mixture over one half of the circle, making sure to leave a clean 10mm (½") rim.
▪ Fold the empty half of the dough over the ingredients and press the outer edges together with your fingers.
▪ Bake for approx. 20 mins in the hottest oven. Check after 10 min, and cover with tin foil if it browns too quickly.
▪ When cooked remove from oven and brush with olive oil.
Serve with the tomato sauce and greens.

CALZONE TAPENADE & GRILLED RED PEPPERS

INGREDIENTS

140g (5oz) basic pizza dough (SEE P. 17)
85g (3oz) Mozzarella, grated
2 tablespoons black olive tapenade (SEE P. 39)
2 red peppers, grilled (SEE P. 35)
25g (1oz) Parmesan, freshly grated
basil oil or olive oil

METHOD

PLACE PIZZA TILE on the floor of the oven and preheat to maximum for one hour.

ASSEMBLING THE CALZONE Stretch the dough into a 20cm (8") circle.
▪ Place the filling over one half of the circle, making sure to leave a clean 10mm (½") rim and then layer one ingredient on top of another.
▪ Begin with a layer of Mozzarella.
▪ Cover with the tapenade, red peppers and Parmesan.
▪ Fold the other half of the dough over the mixture and press the edges together.
▪ Bake for approx. 20 mins in the hottest oven.
▪ Check after 10 mins, and cover with tin foil if it browns too quickly.
▪ Remove from the oven when cooked and brush with basil or olive oil.
Serve with a pesto, or with the basic tomato sauce.

AUBERGINE & HOT SAUSAGE **CALZONE**

INGREDIENTS

140g (5oz) basic pizza dough (SEE P. 17)
1 aubergine
85g (3oz) Mozzarella
225g (8oz) home made hot sausage (SEE P. 86)
3 tablespoons tomato sauce
a good bunch of coriander
50mls (2 fl oz, ¼ cup) hot chilli and tomato sauce (SEE P. 31)

METHOD

PLACE PIZZA TILE on the floor of the oven and preheat to maximum for one hour.

PREPARING THE AUBERGINE
▪ Slice, brush with olive oil and either bake or grill until just cooked.

ASSEMBLING THE CALZONE Stretch the dough into a 20cm (8") circle.
▪ Place the filling over one half of the circle, making sure to leave a clean 10mm (½") rim and then layer one ingredient on top of another.
▪ Begin with a layer of Mozzarella.
▪ Next, add the hot sausage, the tomato sauce, the coriander and finally the sliced aubergines.
▪ Fold the other half of the dough over the mixture and press the edges together.
▪ Bake for approx. 20 mins in the hottest oven.
▪ Check after 10 mins, and cover with tin foil if it browns too quickly.
▪ Remove from the oven when cooked and brush with olive oil.
Serve with tomato and ginger sauce, avocado salsa and a green salad.

STROMBOLI BREAD

This is my very own interpretation of a Sicilian roll, given to me by a native to those parts. It is pure and simple comfort food, ideally served warm. Here I fill it with sautéed vegetables.

INGREDIENTS

140g (5oz) basic pizza dough (SEE P. 17)
2 medium red onions, thinly sliced
olive oil
175g (6oz) mushrooms, sliced
2 cloves garlic, finely chopped
25g (1oz) cream cheese, crumbled
salt and pepper
1 pepper, grilled, skinned & roughly sliced (SEE P. 35)
25g (1oz) Parmesan, freshly grated
2 tablespoons basic tomato sauce (SEE P. 30)

METHOD

PLACE PIZZA TILE on floor of the oven and preheat to maximum for one hour.

PREPARING THE FILLING Sauté the onions in olive oil until translucent.
■ Add the mushrooms and sauté until they too are soft.
■ Add the garlic and sauté again, stirring and shaking the pan all the while.
■ Season with salt and pepper. Allow the ingredients to go completely cold.

ASSEMBLING THE BREAD Stretch the dough into a 20cm (8") circle, place the filling in the centre of the dough, first the vegetable mixture, then the cream cheese, grilled pepper and finally the Parmesan.
■ Working at the right side of the dough, pull up the two "corner" points and pinch it together with the fingers of your left hand.
■ Still holding the pinched-together dough, collect up the tail of dough hanging between, using your right hand, and wrap it around the pinched-together dough, removing your left hand, and pinching now four layers of dough with your right hand.
■ This should enfold around the filling like the prow of a ship.
■ Repeat this process of pinching together two edges of the dough and then lifting and wrapping the tail of dough still hanging, to form a prow at the other side of the dough.
■ The final result should have the dough wrapped around the filling in an ark-like shape – revealing the contents inside.
■ Bake in the preheated oven for approx. 20 mins.
■ A simpler method is to crimp the sides of the dough together, as if forming a pasty, allow a slit in the middle revealing the contents and bake as above.
■ Pour warmed tomato sauce over the cooked bread and serve with a salad – crunchy choy sum shoots are perfect when in season and when available.

PIZZA BAKED BLIND

This came about from just experimenting with a good pizza dough, brushing it with oil, maybe a little garlic and putting it in the oven to cook and *then* topping it rather than the other way round. It is a great pre-baked bread, super as a picnic food, taking all the condiments along separately, and it's wonderful around the grill with barbecued fish and vegetables. Or, you can bake it there and then, just take it out, top it, slice it and eat it.

It's completely different to a pizza. It's much crisper and more defined...

SERVING SUGGESTIONS

1. Spread a heaped tablespoon of crème fraîche on the pizza, drape with smoked salmon and thinly sliced red onion. Drizzle with hot chilli oil and serve with a wedge of lemon.

2. Spread a few tablespoons of caramelised garlic on the pizza. Add oven roasted black pepper tomatoes, quartered, and shavings of parmigiano reggiano.

3. Spread basil pesto on the pizza and completely cover with a layer of roasted pine nuts.

4. In a bowl mix together a tablespoon of sun-dried tomato pesto with a tablespoon of crème fraîche. Spread on top of pizza with torn rocket leaves.

5. Top the pizza with 2 table-spoons of sour cream, cover with a lattice of roasted red peppers. In between the lattice place herbed olives and capers.

6. Spread a generous layer of black olive tapenade on the pizza. Arrange cloves of roast garlic on top and sprinkle with hot paprika and a drizzle of basil oil.

7. Warm some ratatouille and spoon generously onto the pizza. Serve garnished with fresh basil leaves.

8. Spread aubergine purée on the pizza. Top with 5 or 6

IT'S A CRISP PIECE OF DOUGH ONTO WHICH YOU ADD FLAVOURINGS AND WHAT YOU TOP IT WITH IS USUALLY COLD, APART FROM A WARM RATATOUILLE

PIZZA BAKED BLIND LOVES SAUCES intense sauces like tapenade, pesto, pepper and almond, there is no end to what the imagination can do if it has those toppings together, it's a field day of flavour and colour, real summer food.
But it can be winter food as well, with a bowl of soup, and with root vegetables.

TO BAKE PIZZA BLIND simply take 140g (5oz) pizza dough and stretch it to a 20cm (8") circle.
▪ Brush with a light coat of olive oil and bake in a preheated 500°F, 240°C, Gas 9 oven for approx. 6 mins to a light golden brown crust.
▪ Turn over once or twice during cooking. Remove from the oven and place ingredients on top. Slice and serve.

ALTERNATIVE Pizza baked blind can be made in advance and kept wrapped in a tea cloth. To re-heat place in a hot oven for about 1 min. Brush with olive oil and place ingredients on top.

anchovies and black olives.

9. Combine parmesan, fresh garlic and basil with toasted pine nuts and place on top of some tomato and ginger sauce on the pizza.

10. Spread on some onion confit and garnish with pomegranate seeds and fresh chervil.

11. Dress simply with fresh basil and top quality olive oil.

12. Spread two tablespoons of aubergine purée onto the pizza, sprinkle over dillisk crisps and grate the zest of half a lemon on top.

13. Combine 1 tablespoon of sun-dried tomato pesto with a tablespoon of homemade pesto. Spread on the pizza and place diced roasted red pepper and diced olives in segments on top.

14. Spread Fava Bean Cream on the pizza. Top with strips of sun-dried tomatoes and shaved pecorino.

15. Soak 20g (3/4 oz) fresh ginger, julienned, for an hour in ice cold water. Julienne 25g (1oz) baby leeks (white part only) to the length of a matchstick. Onto your blind pizza, spread 3 tablespoons of thick creamy yoghurt. Arrange leek and ginger matchsticks. Flake 115g (4oz) smoked tuna over. Serve with the lemon.

BRANDADE WITH PEPPER & ALMOND SAUCE

INGREDIENTS

140g (5oz) pizza dough (SEE P. 17)
450g (1lb) salted cod (or ling)
2-3 potatoes, boiled
225mls (8fl oz, 1 cup) crème fraîche
125ml (4fl oz, 1/2 cup) olive oil
7 cloves garlic
Pepper and Almond Sauce (SEE P 39)

METHOD

PLACE PIZZA TILE on the floor of the oven and preheat to maximum for one hour.

MAKING THE BRANDADE Soak the cod overnight, changing the water two to three times.

- Cover the fish with cold water and bring up to a simmer over a medium heat.
- As soon as it reaches simmering point remove and let it stand for about fifteen minutes.
- Scald the crème fraîche by bringing it to boiling point and then take off the heat.
- Cream the cod, garlic and potatoes in the food processor.
- Stream in the olive oil and the scalded crème fraîche.

ASSEMBLING THE PIZZA Stretch the dough into a 20cm (8") circle.

- Bake blind as directed on page 102.
- When ready to serve, spread with the brandade, and garnish with a generous circle of Pepper and Almond Sauce.

SMOKED HADDOCK BRANDADE

INGREDIENTS

140g (5oz) pizza dough (SEE P. 17)
225g (8oz) smoked haddock
milk
1 head fennel
vegetable stock
2 cloves of garlic
scant 50ml (2 fl oz, 1/2 cup) crème fraîche, scalded (see previous recipe)
2 tablespoons warm olive oil
1 tablespoon lemon juice
1 small boiled potato (optional)

METHOD

PLACE PIZZA TILE on the floor of the oven and preheat to maximum for one hour.

MAKING THE BRANDADE Warm a little milk in a shallow saucepan.

- Place the haddock in the warm milk and cook for about 3 mins until the skin comes away.
- When able to handle peel off the skin. Slice the fennel – reserving a few shavings as a garnish – and bake in a little stock until tender.
- Place the garlic and crème fraîche in a mortar and gently crush, using a pestle.
- Add the haddock, the fennel and the potato.
- Drizzle in the warm oil while you pound to a desired consistency. Season with salt and black pepper to taste.

ASSEMBLING THE PIZZA Stretch the dough into a 20cm (8") circle.

- Bake blind as directed on page 102.

When ready to serve, spread the brandade and top with very finely shaved fennel.

OPPOSITE: PIZZA BAKED BLIND WITH COD BANDADE, OVERLEAF: ROD ALSTON OF EDEN PLANTS

PIZZETTES

PIZZETTES ARE SMALLER PIZZAS

They are usually served in the north of Italy at lunch time.

They are quicker to make because of their size, and a pizzette also allows a little extravagance such as the odd truffle shaving and are great for creating a little mezze on the one plate.

At lunchtime I would typically serve a pizzette with onion confit and goat's cheese, a small green salad and a few spiced olives.

OPPOSITE: PIZZETTES

TOMATO & GINGER PIZZETTE

55g (2oz) basic pizza dough (SEE P. 17)
1 tablespoon tomato and ginger sauce (SEE P. 30)
25g (1oz) cream cheese
15g (½ oz) shaved Parmesan, freshly grated
2 oven roasted tomatoes, sliced into 8 pieces
shaved Parmesan for serving
fresh coriander or chervil

PLACE PIZZA TILE on the floor of the oven and preheat to maximum for one hour.

ASSEMBLING THE PIZZETTE

- Stretch the dough into a 9cm (3½") circle, spread on the sauce, the cream cheese, the Parmesan and then the tomatoes.
- Bake in the preheated oven for approx. 6 mins. Serve garnished with shaved Parmesan and fresh herbs.

COURGETTE PIZZETTE

55g (2oz) basic pizza dough (SEE P. 17)
15g (½ oz) Mozzarella, grated
25g (1oz) courgette, slivered and sautéed until soft
a few strips of Parma ham

PLACE PIZZA TILE on the floor of the oven and preheat to maximum for one hour.

ASSEMBLING THE PIZZETTE

- Stretch the dough into a 9cm (3½") circle, sprinkle over the Mozzarella.
- Top with the courgette and Parma.
- Bake in the preheated oven for approx. 6 mins.
- Serve garnished with shaved Parmesan and fresh herbs.

CARAMELISED GARLIC PIZZETTE

55g (2oz) basic pizza dough (SEE P. 17)
1 tablespoon caramelised garlic (SEE P. 34)
1 sun-dried tomato, sliced
15g (½ oz) Stilton

PLACE PIZZA TILE on the floor of the oven and preheat to maximum for one hour.

ASSEMBLING THE PIZZETTE

- Stretch the dough into a 9cm (3½") circle, spread over the garlic.
- Top with tomato and cheese.
- Bake in the preheated oven for approx. 6 mins.

SMOKED TROUT PIZZETTE

55g (2oz) basic pizza dough (SEE P. 17)
1 tablespoon basic tomato sauce (SEE P. 30)
15g (1/2 oz) cream cheese, crumbled
25g (1 oz) smoked trout, carefully broken into pieces
capers

PLACE PIZZA TILE on the floor of the oven and preheat to maximum for one hour.

ASSEMBLING THE PIZZETTE

- Stretch the dough into a 9cm (3 1/2") circle, spread on the tomato sauce, the cream cheese, trout and capers.
- Bake in the preheated oven for approx. 6 mins.

PESTO PIZZETTE

55g (2oz) basic pizza dough (SEE P. 17)
1 tablespoon home made pesto (SEE P. 40)
15g (1/2 oz) goat's cheese
3 black olives

PLACE PIZZA TILE on the floor of the oven and preheat to maximum for one hour.

ASSEMBLING THE PIZZETTE

- Stretch the dough into a 9cm (3 1/2") circle, spread on the pesto.
- Top with goat's cheese and olives.
- Bake in the preheated oven for approx. 6 mins.

PEAR & CAVIAR PIZZETTE

55g (2oz) basic pizza dough (SEE P. 17)
1 tablespoon Mascarpone
1 poached pear
1 generous teaspoon Caviar

PLACE PIZZA TILE on the floor of the oven and preheat to maximum for one hour.

ASSEMBLING THE PIZZETTE

- Stretch the dough into a 9cm (3 1/2") circle, lightly spread on half the Mascarpone.
- Arrange the pear on top and place the Caviar in the centre.
- Bake in the preheated oven for approx. 6 mins.
- Dot with the remaining Mascarpone and serve.

FOCACCIA

ONE OF THE GREAT FLATBREADS

COOKED DOWN AMONG THE ASHES FLAVOURED WITH HERBS AND OIL. IT'S BASICALLY A WELL SEASONED BREAD SERVED AS A SNACK, PART OF THE MEAL OR MEZZE TABLE

Sometimes made in a pan,

and sometimes on a pizza stone,

FOCACCIA is always characterized

by its dimples, a simple technique of

pressing the tips of your fingers into the

dough, creating holes

which catch little pools of olive oil and

sea salt which permeate the dough.

BASIC FOCACCIA

INGREDIENTS

1 dough recipe, sponge method (SEE P. 22)
2-3 very ripe tomatoes, thinly sliced
½ teaspoon of salt
2 cloves garlic, minced
2 tablespoons of olive oil
¼ teaspoon of dried oregano
6 basil leaves, finely julienned
25g (1 oz) Parmesan, grated

METHOD

FOLLOW THE SPONGE DOUGH RECIPE on page 22.

PREHEAT THE OVEN TO ITS MAXIMUM TEMPERATURE.

PUNCH DOWN THE DOUGH

- Oil a 23cm (9") pan (either square or round, the shape is irrelevant) and press in the dough.
- Cover the pan with cling film and allow the dough to rest for 30 mins.
- Dimple the dough with your fingers. Place the tomatoes in a single layer on top and sprinkle over all the other ingredients.
- Bake in the preheated oven for approx. 20 mins.
- Serve warm, drizzled with olive oil, or a flavoured oil, or the oil from sun-dried tomatoes.

Alternative toppings are fennel seeds; anchovies; or stoned olives, salt and garlic; or simply coarse salt and garlic with olive oil.

POTATO & ROSEMARY FOCACCIA

INGREDIENTS

1 recipe Potato and Rosemary Focaccia Dough (SEE P. 23)
sea salt
paper thin slices of 1-2 medium onions
olive oil
rosemary oil

METHOD

FOLLOW THE SPONGE DOUGH RECIPE on page 22.

PREHEAT THE OVEN TO ITS MAXIMUM TEMPERATURE.

PUNCH DOWN THE DOUGH

- Oil two 20cm (8") baking trays and press in the dough.

(Or use 700g (1lb 9oz) dough in a standard 15cm x 23 cm (6"x 9") baking tray and make focaccia sandwiches with the remaining dough.

- Cover with cling film and allow to rise for an hour.
- Dimple the dough with your fingers and sprinkle with sea salt and onion slices (making sure not to overlap).
- Drizzle with olive oil and bake on the bottom shelf of the oven for 20-25mins until golden brown on top and bottom.
- Check after 15mins & cover with foil if the onions are browning
- Remove onto a wire rack.
- Serve warm with rosemary oil.

THE FOCACCIA SANDWICH

Sliced and packed with delicious ingredients focaccia makes amazing sandwiches.

INGREDIENTS

For each sandwich use 140g (5oz) pizza dough, sponge method (SEE P. 22)

METHOD

- Place the pizza tile in the oven and preheat to its maximum temperature.
- Press down the prepared dough with the palm of your hand to flatten to no more than 10cm-13cm (4"-5") circumference.
- Allow to rest for 10 mins.
- Dimple down the dough and scatter with coarsely ground sea salt.
- Drizzle with olive oil.
- Use a pizza peel to place onto the hot pizza tile and bake for approx. 7 mins, until golden brown.

Instead of olive oil, you can drizzle the dough with a flavoured oil, such as basil oil before cooking.

RED CABBAGE WITH DILLISK SANDWICH

basil oil
85g (3oz) goat's quark or soft cream goat's cheese
1 tablespoon ground dillisk (SEE P. 123)
115g (4oz) red cabbage casserole, cooked
5 leaves purple basil
a good bunch of cress
15g (½oz) dillisk crisps (SEE P. 123)

METHOD

- When baking the focaccia dimple basil oil into the dough (see above).
- Combine the quark or cream cheese with the ground dillisk.
- Make the sandwich with the cheese, the cabbage, the basil leaves, cress and the dillisk crisps on top.

AUBERGINE & APRICOT SANDWICH

40g (1½oz) cream cheese
15g (½oz) pine nuts, toasted in the oven
a little grated nutmeg
3 dried apricots
3 thin slices of baked aubergine
1 tablespoon crème fraîche
a little Corsican mint

METHOD

- Place the cream cheese, pine nuts, nutmeg and apricots in a food processor and process until almost smooth.
- Make the sandwich with the cream cheese mixture, the aubergine, crème fraîche and mint.

SANDWICH IDEAS

SALAMI & SUN-DRIED TOMATO

pepper and almond sauce
generous spread of sour cream
provencal salami
sun-dried tomatoes, torn into strips
Spread the sour cream over the bottom half of the focaccia, add the salami, the sauce and top with the tomatoes.

SMOKED HADDOCK WITH PEPPER & ALMOND SAUCE

crème fraîche
pepper and almond sauce
smoked haddock, sliced very thinly
scallions, diced
crisp lettuce
Combine the crème fraîche with the sauce and spread on the bottom half of the focaccia. Top with haddock, scallions and the best quality crisp lettuce.

ROQUEFORT & SUN-DRIED TOMATO

Roquefort
sun-dried tomato
walnuts, toasted and broken into pieces
Choy-sum shoots
Layer the ingredients starting with the cheese, the tomatoes, the walnuts and then the shoots.

OVEN ROASTED TOMATOES & FAVA BEAN CREAM

fava bean cream
oven roasted tomatoes
torn basil leaves
freshly grated Pecorino
mixed salad leaves
Layer the ingredients starting with the fava bean cream, then the tomatoes, basil, cheese and salad leaves.

GABRIEL CHEESE & OVEN ROASTED TOMATO SAUCE

wedge of Gabriel cheese
oven roasted tomato sauce
handful of lambs lettuce
handful of purslane
Layer the ingredients beginning with the Gabriel, the sauce, and then the leaves.

GREEN OLIVE TAPENADE & RED PEPPER

green olive tapenade
red pepper, roasted
hand-rolled Mozzarella, freshly sliced
Spread the tapenade on the base and top with the pepper and the cheese.

PESTO & BAKED AUBERGINE

home-made pesto
sliced baked aubergine
olive oil
rocket leaves
Brush the aubergine slices with the olive oil and bake in the oven until they are brown and just soft.
Spread the pesto on the base of the sandwich and top with aubergine and rocket leaves. Drizzle over olive oil

TOMATO, CARAMELIZED GARLIC & FETA

tomatoes
olive oil
salt and pepper
caramelized garlic
Feta cheese
mixed greens
Peel, seed and chop the tomatoes, toss them in the oil, salt and pepper. Spread the caramelized garlic on the base of the sandwich and top with tomatoes, Feta and mixed greens.

DURRUS, AUBERGINE & BELGIAN ENDIVE

Durrus Cheese (or smoked Durrus where available)
baked aubergine slices
Belgian endive
Brush the aubergine slices with the olive oil and bake in the oven until they are brown and just soft. Layer the sandwich with the aubergine, Durrus and the endive.

HERBED SOFT GOAT'S QUARK WITH PEPPER & ALMOND SAUCE

Garlic and Herbed Goat's Quark, or garlic and herbed goat's cream cheese
salt and freshly ground black pepper
flat leaf parsley
pepper and almond sauce
Spread the base with the cheese, season and finish with parsley and finally the sauce.

OPPOSITE: FOCACCIA SANDWICH WITH RED CABBAGE & DILLISK. OVERLEAF: BERNADETTE'S SALAD

RELISHES

THESE DISTINCTIVE AND HIGHLY FLAVOURED DISHES ARE SERVED ON THE SIDE. THEY COMPLETE THE MEAL BECAUSE THEY GIVE CONTRAST. CARRAGEEN MOSS AND PEACH RELISH WITH HOT SAUSAGE PIZZA; HOT CHILLI OIL WITH A SPINACH PIZZA; GINGER AND TOMATO RELISH WITH A CALZONE, THESE CONTRASTS ADD COLOUR AND LIFE TO A MEAL, THE FLAVOURS BOUNCING OFF EACH OTHER, AWAKENING THE TASTE BUDS.

IT WAS JEAN-GEORGES VONGERICHTEN WHO INTRODUCED THE WORLD TO INFUSED OILS – VERY SIMPLE TO MAKE – THE OIL ABSORBS THE FLAVOUR OF THE INGREDIENT USED.

DRIZZLED OVER A PIZZA, FOCACCIA OR CALZONE IT MAKES THE WORLD OF DIFFERENCE.

OVERLEAF: DILLISK – FRESH, DRIED, CRISPED & GROUND. OPPOSITE: FLAVOURED OILS (SEE P. 122)

HOT CHILLI OIL

450ml (16 fl oz, 2 cups) of vegetable oil, 25g (1oz, 1/2 cup) small dried red chillies

- Heat the oil and fry chillies in it until almost black.
- Turn off the heat. Cool and then store.
- This oil lasts forever, well at least for a year.
- Optional additions are a cinnamon stick, a few cloves and/or whole peppercorns.
- This oil can be drizzled onto any pizza.

ROSEMARY OIL

25g (1oz, 1/2 cup) rosemary leaves, very finely minced in food processor, 200ml (8 fl oz, 1 cup) olive oil

- Combine the oil and chopped herb in a jar.
- Shake well and allow to stand at room temperature for 2-3 hours.
- Refrigerated it will last for 3-4 weeks.
- Alternatively heat oil and rosemary (stems included) in a saucepan.
- Bring to boil. Allow to simmer a further 7-8 minutes then store in the fridge.
- This method lasts for about a week.

BASIL OIL

70g (2 1/2 oz, 2 1/2 cups) basil leaves, 300ml (10 fl oz, 1 1/4 cups) olive oil

- Blanch the basil for a least 7 or 8 seconds in boiling water and chill immediately in a bowl of iced water.
- Allow the herbs to drain and then pat dry with a tea cloth.
- Place in a food processor/liquidiser and blend.
- Drizzle in the olive oil blending until well combined.
- Put the oil into a clean jar, store in the fridge and allow the herbs to settle.
- In the morning filter through a cheesecloth (ladle from top), tea towel, or dampened coffee filter (the slowest method).
- It is now ready for use and will keep for about 8 days in the fridge.

SPICY OLIVES

2 tablespoons olive oil
1/4 teaspoon caraway seeds
115g (4oz) black olives
1/4 teaspoon cumin seeds
hot pepper flakes to taste
1 clove garlic, very thinly sliced
few strips of lemon rind/zest
1 tablespoon chopped parsley
50ml (2 fl oz, 1/4 cup) lemon juice

- Toast the cumin seeds until they give off a lemony aroma.
- Grind with the caraway seeds in a pestle and mortar.
- Combine all the ingredients except the parsley and let stand for at least an hour.
- Mix in the parsley and serve.

OVEN ROASTED TOMATO RELISH

12 oven roasted tomatoes, roughly diced
1 small red onion, diced
10 olives, stoned and chopped
1 teaspoon capers
50ml (2 fl oz, 1/4 cup) olive oil
50ml (2 fl oz, 1/4 cup) balsamic vinegar
10 basil leaves finely sliced

- Combine all the ingredients together.
- This will keep for weeks if kept tightly covered in a jar and stored in the fridge.

AVOCADO & CORIANDER RELISH

2 avocados, stoned and cubed
1 large red onion, finely chopped
4 tomatoes, chopped
25g (1oz, ½ cup) coriander, chopped
1 green chilli, chopped (optional)
2½ dessertspoons balsamic vinegar
ground black pepper to taste
sea salt (optional)

- In a bowl, coat the avocado with the vinegar.
- Add remaining ingredients.
- Gently mix.
- Serve as soon as it's made.

FRESH PEACH WITH CARRAGEEN RELISH

15g (½ oz) carrageen seaweed
450ml (16 fl oz) water
50ml (2 fl oz, ¼ cup) of raspberry coulis (see below)
1 red onion, diced
1 red pepper, diced
1 red chilli thinly sliced
juice of 2 limes
3 tablespoons of chopped coriander
salt and freshly ground black pepper to taste
5 medium sized peaches, roughly diced

- Check through the carrageen for shells and small stones and wash carefully.
- Place in a saucepan with the water and soak for 30 minutes.
- Bring to the boil and simmer for about an hour.
- Meanwhile make the raspberry coulis
- Heat a generous handful of raspberries over a medium heat until pulpy, then push through a fine sieve with a pestle.
- Towards the end of the carrageen cooking time, begin to prepare the other ingredients (except the peaches) and combine in a bowl.
- After an hour of cooking strain the carrageen liquid into a clean bowl and allow to partially cool while you prepare and add the peaches to the mixture.
- Before the carageen sets add it too to the fruit mixture and gently combine.
- Cover and refrigerate.

TOASTED DILLISK CRISPS

Dillisk crisps are terrific for sandwiches, the final addition to a salad, as a garnish, as part of an antipasti platter, with smoked salmon, or simply as a snack food. As a condiment, ground dillisk is a wonderful replacement for salt, use on everything from a boiled egg to a soup, even in porridge.

- Place dillisk onto the hot pizza tile in an oven preheated to its maximum temperature.
- Toast for about 5 mins, until crisp.
- To make a ground dillisk condiment, finely grind the toasted dillisk to a powder using a pestle and mortar.

GLOSSARY & MAIL ORDER

BALSAMIC VINEGAR

Spend money on a real, aged, Balsamic, which is admittedly very expensive, but a little goes a long way. Of the varieties currently available the extra aged Mazzetti product is good for daily use.

CHEESE FROM IRISH FARMHOUSES

Irish farmhouse cheeses have been one of the glories of the renaissance of Irish food, and are indispensable for making exciting pizzas.
The farmhouse cheeses used for pizzas in this book are Smoked Gubbeen, a semi-hard, cow's cheese, made in south west Cork by Gianna and Tom Ferguson, and smoked by neighbour Chris Jepson; Cashel Blue, made by Jane and Louis Grubb, a creamy blue veined cheese from Tipperary; Milleens, from Veronica Steele, a pungent semi-soft cheese from the Beara Peninsula in Co Cork; St Tola Goat's Log, made by Meg and Derrick Gordon, a fine goat's cheese from Co Clare; Cooleeney, made by Breda Maher, a milky Camembert-type cheese from the boggy lands of Co Tipperary and Cratloe Hills Sheep's Cheese, made by Sean and Deirdre Fitzgerald, a sheep's cheese from Co Limerick – always buy the mature variety which is labelled as such.
In the sandwiches I use Durrus, a herby semi-soft cheese made by Jeffa Gill in Co Cork and Bill Hogan's Gabriel, a beautifully made Gruyère-type cheese from near Schull in Co Cork.

FLOUR

For the basic pizza dough I always use an organic unbleached strong flour made from hard wheat. Irish all purpose flour is generally too soft, has less texture and flavour, but is wonderful for cakes and biscuits! To produce a pizza on a commercial basis the flour must have at least a 1410 gluten content which accounts for its ability to rise and its strength when stretched into very thin circles of dough.
The organic wholemeal flour which I use in the wholemeal base is difficult to work with because it absorbs so much moisture but the nutty texture is well worth the effort.
Spelt, which I was first introduced to in Puglia, is an ancient strain of wheat, and because its structure has never been scientifically altered, it is often used by people who have allergies to other wheat strains. You can find this flour in most healthfood shops.
In the Potato and Rosemary dough for Focaccia, I combine this with Durum flour which is not very widely available, but you can find it in specialist Italian shops. Wholefood shops usually sell a "Pasta & Pizza" flour mix, which is a mixture of durum flour with blended wheat.

GORGONZOLA

From Lombardy in Italy, this is a cow's milk blue cheese, soft with a very powerful smell. It can be bought either *dolce,* sweet, young, soft or *naturale,* more aged and firm with a sharper flavour. Infrequently used in cooking in Ireland, but becoming more available. Delis and supermarkets sell it, but the best will be found in specialised cheese suppliers.

MASCARPONE

Very soft, full fat, and creamy, Mascarpone originates from Lombardy. Made with cow's milk, it is not in fact, by definition, a cheese, as no starter or rennet is used in its production. Mascarpone is now widely available in shops and supermarkets.

MOZZARELLA

I always place the Mozzarella on the bottom layer of a pizza, just over the sauce (if using sauce) because it contains quite a bit of moisture and it is more likely to brown quickly. It also tends to form a sort of lining for the pizza preventing the other ingredients from making the pizza crust soggy. When it melts it draws the other ingredients together making them more stable and compact, and helps to prevent what is known as Pizza Slide. For most pizza recipes in this book buy Irish Mozzarella in a block, and grate it yourself. But, where specified in a particular recipe, look out for hand rolled fresh Mozzarella made from cow's milk.
Real Mozzarella comes from Campania in Southern Italy *Mozzarella di bufala,* made from the milk of water buffalos.

OLIVE OIL, FLAVOURED OILS AND MARINADES

When making a herb or chilli flavoured oil it is not necessary to use an Extra Virgin Olive oil, Pure

Olive Oil is more appropriate, given that the flavour of the herb will dominate. I give three recipes for flavoured oils in this book, but I also recommend the West Cork Herb flavoured oils, marinades, and mustards available in some supermarkets and from West Cork Herb Farm, Church Cross, Skibbereen, Co Cork.

OLIVES

My preferred olive is the classic Niçoise or good Kalamata, but look out for Amphissa which is a Greek olive which can be found in good Delis or from Toby Simmonds of The Real Olive Co., who runs market stalls all over the country.
Avoid olives that have seasonings added – buy olives in oil rather than brine and add your own prepared seasoning. If you find an olive you like ask for the name of it. Simply knowing the country is not enough. I also recommend dry roasted olives.

PARMESAN

Always use Parmigiano Reggiano, its nutty flavour cannot be rivalled. The name Parmigiano Reggiano is always stamped on the wheel of the cheese, so make sure to get the real thing, and not Grana Padano. Use the rind of the cheese, scraped clean, for soups, stews and sauces.

PECORINO ROMANO

Not widely available but can be found in a specialist deli. It is a sheep's milk cheese, and one of the most popular cheeses in Italy, though it originated in Sardinia.
If you cannot find this cheese use Cratloe Sheep's Cheese from Co Limerick

PEPPERONI

This spicy sausage is commonly available in supermarkets and delis. Make sure to buy dried pepperoni. Always avoid vac-packed pepperoni. Smoked pepperoni is also recommended.

PICKLED GINGER

Slivers of fresh ginger in a pickling brine.
To be found in Asian Stores.

PORCINI

Italian dried mushrooms, used when reconstituted. Widely available, buy the best you can afford.

RICOTTA SALATA

An off-white dense, salted sheep's milk curd cheese, available from good Deli counters. If you can't find it substitute a Greek Feta cheese.

SALAD LEAVES

Starter, main course, side dish, light and dark green, tender and leafed with a grassy bitter-sweet crunch, the green salad knows no bounds.
At the restaurant I used up to 30 ingredients in just one salad and that's without the dressing. In fact the dressing was used in spartan amounts.
I always combine a mixture of compatible leaves for flavour: bittersweet, spicy, hot, perfumed, grassy; for texture: soft, crunchy, curly, silky. Buy a minimum of four heads for a salad mesclun, a mix. Avoid the packaged mesclun variety which is generally imported, non organic and well off peak condition. When buying a head of lettuce turn it over and look at the stem: it will be off white if freshly cut, brown if sitting for days. Buy lettuce which is crisp and tightly packed. If there is a trace of brown on

"At the restaurant I used up to 30 ingredients in just one salad
and that's without the dressing.
In fact the dressing was used in spartan amounts."

the inner leaves, or the outer leaves droop and have lost their moisture, put it back. Ask the storekeeper about the harvesting, when was it picked? Is it local? Who is the grower? When is the delivery day – which is really the day to buy. Above all else, is it organic?
Only buy organic. Lettuce is the most maligned little creature. It has such a short life that making its shelf life longer is the sole goal of commercial growers, so they spray and feed it to death with very nasty chemicals which actually change the flavour, alter the texture, and interfere with the colour of the food. The taste is ghastly, and pesticide residues are often considerable. To be avoided at all costs.

FRESH HERBS

I usually choose soft herbs, such as golden marjoram, basil, mint, Italian parsley (flat leaf parsley), coriander, oregano, marjoram and the tender tip leaves of lemon thyme, finely chopped chives, and full chive shoots. Use a damp cloth to wipe off any earth which may have lodged on the herbs, pluck the leaves into a bowl. Toss all the herbs into the salad just before the dressing is added.

CLEANING THE LETTUCE

It is important to avoid bruising the lettuce leaves when cleaning. Gently rub clean any sand or grit with your thumbs under cold running water. Dry in very small amounts in a salad spinner, being careful not to overspin.
Tear evenly into large bite-size pieces, discarding some of the long or hard stalks. Using your hands, combine gently the lettuce with the herbs in a large bowl – add the dressing sparingly – just enough to coat the leaves. Arrange handfuls of the salad in the centre of plates, build on this stack using lighter amounts as you get to the top. Decorate the salad with long chives, sliced ruby chard stalks, purslane leaves, edible flowers and an extra sprinkle of herbs. All of this must be done at high speed or the salad leaves will wilt. In Napoli and other parts of Italy the salad is arranged first and dressed afterwards. It is usually dressed with a fruity olive oil and a squeeze of lemon, no more than that.

The salad ingredients used in the photo on page 118 are: Mizuna; Cress; Choy Sum leaves and shoots; Wild and Salad Rocket; Swiss Chard; Ruby Chard; Mint; Sage; Winter Purslane; Shungiku; Wall Valerian; Flat Leaf Parsley; Lemon Thyme; Variegated Thyme; Golden Thyme; Japanese Parsley; Endive; Butterhead Lettuce; Raddiccio; Lollo Biondi; Red Oak Lettuce; Pea Shoots; Oregano Leaves; Chives; Pot Marjoram; Golden Marjoram; Coriander; Garlic Chives; Flowers from Triangular Stalked Garlic, Cowslips, Viola, Primroses and Borage.

SALAMI

I always buy the hairy herbacious French salami. It always contains a huge meat percentage. A good thick, black-pepper crusted Italian salami is also great, generally stocked in a good Deli.

SALT

The most commonly available salt is the iodized commercial variety. The best salt to use for the dough is Fine Sea Salt. Coarse Sea Salt is used to sprinkle on the top of focaccia.

SMOKED FISH

There are many wonderful smokers in Ireland. Having used Sally Barnes' Woodcock Smokery wild smoked salmon, haddock and mussels, I found there was no going back. Its full, rounded soft, buttery smoked flavour makes it so distinctive. Mail order from: Woodcock Smokery, Gortbrea, Castletownshend,
Co Cork. Tel: 028-36232.
Also from Cork, look out for the gorgeous smoked mussels, salmon and eel made by Frank Hederman in Cobh. Mail order from: Belvelley, Cobh, Co Cork Tel: 021-811089

TOMATOES

Even in Naples, famous for its tomatoes, I found them using canned plum tomatoes for the pizza sauce. I always buy plum tomatoes which have been canned with basil leaves. Dublin's Little Italy shop sell a PAC pomodori pelati which I find quite good. When using fresh tomatoes look out for home-grown varieties and avoid the commonly available Dutch tomatoes. Some of the Spanish imported tomatoes are a very good quality. Organic tomatoes must always be a first preference when available. But Italian plum tomatoes are simply the best.

YEAST

I always use fresh yeast, and it is worth making an effort to find it. Alternatively, and as a last resort, use active dry baker's yeast. Avoid the "quick rise" variety which forces the dough to rise in half the time – you also lose half the flavour and texture

INDEX

INDEX